Pra

RANDY'S WAY

"You must read *Randy's Way* to believe it. Randy and Kim Hebert share their story of love for God, family, and friends, as they uncover intimate details of their personal struggles with ALS. Find out how over twelve million minutes in "locked in syndrome" has not limited Randy nor Kim in helping others as active contributors to their church, community, and society."

~ Clay Olsen, Pastor, Chapel by The Sea, Emerald Isle

"I have known Randy and Kim since we were young Marine officers and Generals' aides. Well written from the heart, *Randy's Way* inspires readers to overcome any challenge they face."

~ Mike Braham, Healthcare Executive, Men's Ministry Leader, Marine Corps Harrier Pilot

***

Donations to continue research to find a cure for ALS may be made to: The ALS Association, North Carolina Chapter, 4 North Blount Street, Suite 200, Raleigh, NC 27601

Thomas P. Gill

When Kim asked Randy if he thought they would survive, he gave her peace in saying, "We have constant blessings" and "God will provide."

****

For more than twenty-three years, Randy Hebert has lived as a physical prisoner of war with a disease that ravages his body but can't touch his soul. If you meet him today, you will observe his spirit radiate until your eyes no longer notice the highly decorated Marine officer is a wheelchair bound, physical shell of the hero he once was, a man who now lives with the life-threatening, debilitating effects of one of the worst diseases known to man. But Major Randy Hebert refuses to surrender to self-pity, doesn't whine, and doesn't give up. How? It's Randy's Way-God's plan-a true story to tell your children.

****

Running through the tree-covered undulating terrain of Fort Leonard Wood, Missouri was one of my favorite past times. The small hills of the Missouri Ozarks offer just enough challenge. To make it more intense, I simply add more miles; not unlike living at Emerald Isle, North Carolina as a young Marine when I would keep on running to make up for the flat, but visually stimulating seascape. Sometimes I would run in the sand and water to make it even more challenging – Oohrah!

Not today.

In the Spring of 1995, my Commanding Officer and our Sergeant Major decided to go for a run. We didn't have a particular route in mind and when we reached an intersection I decided to go straight instead of turning left and enduring a mile and half steep hill. I didn't know at the time that my choice, the base perimeter road, was nine miles long and sported its own steep hill. I started out fine but wasn't mentally prepared for how my body was going to react to the run. Instead of pushing the pace, I quickly began to drag. Colonel Smith gave me grief the entire run as I struggled to stay with them.

When we crested the steep hill, we stopped for water in a nearby office. As we started running again, my legs felt even heavier and I was soaking wet from the humidity, yet I fought to keep my knees moving. For the first time in my life I wondered if I would make it. There was only a half mile left but I was almost out of gas. I didn't want to admit that ALS, which one of the doctor's suspected was my condition, was already affecting my physical body.

Shuffling onward – if I stopped I wouldn't get started again - I saw her. Just ahead, no more than a hundred yards was my beautiful bride of three years, Kim. Was this a mirage? I knew I was tired, but really – that beat?

Why would Kim be driving on this side of the fort with the kids?

Only the training schools and military ranges were over here making it an ideal place to run.

Who cares?

Thankfully, she saw me as I waved her down to pick me up. Nearly collapsing, I opened the car door and heard her say,

"Get in and I'll drive."

Although not too unusual for *my* wife, as most military men know, *that* is almost never going to happen, especially with kids in the car. But then I saw my beautiful babies, Nicole and Kyle, sitting in the back seat, and nearly crumpled.

I complied.

Kim ran the air full blast. This was painfully and obviously the last straw. I had been complaining privately, while publicly hiding my illness, for too long. What might have happened if Kim had not been there? We'll never know. In retrospect, and believe me I wouldn't have said this twenty-three years ago, but this was God's work! He placed my angel on that road.

RANDY'S WAY

A MARINE'S FAITH-BASED JOURNEY WITH ALS

Thomas P. Gill

Published by CreateSpace Publishing, March 2018

Published in the United States of America

ISBN: 978-1985380004

Library of Congress Control Number: 2018902140

For our parents, siblings, friends, and

especially our two wonderful children

Nicole Elizabeth Hebert

&

Kyle Eugene Hebert

FOREWORD

With deference to those who hesitate to acknowledge the importance of religion and faith in everyday life, particularly when that life confronts you with unimaginable challenges, *Randy's Way* is a must read for anyone interested in studying the lives of real-life heroes and heroines and learning how they earned their titles. The book tells the story of a dynamic, "high potential" Marine Corps officer who selflessly exchanged his quality of life for a role in the Gulf War and who, in so doing, began to cultivate a closer, hand-in-hand walk with God. Kim, Randy's wife of three years at the time, never wavered in her devotion to Randy, even when given the devastating news that her gifted and athletic husband had contracted ALS as a result of the Gulf War's toxic cocktail. The epic account of events leading up to that life-altering moment and the twenty-five years that followed gives new meaning to the phrase, "courage under fire." I have known Randy for more than thirty years, ever since I hand-picked this confident young Marine officer to serve as my "Aide-de-camp" at the 2nd Marine Air Wing in Havelock, North Carolina. Enjoy this inspiring example of how to keep your faith strong while being faithful and resilient as a husband and father, in spite of overwhelming challenges.

Brigadier General John C. Arick, USMC, Retired

CONTENTS

FOREWORD

INVITATION

AUTHOR'S THOUGHTS

PART ONE: IN THE BEGINNING

1. Made for the Movies – "Take One"

2. *Young Frankenstein*

3. My D-Day

4. "Always do right-this will gratify some and astonish the rest."

5. Family Jewels

6. "I never let my best friend do stupid things…alone."

7. Bad Hand

8. "One for all, and all for one."

9. Wild Man

10. The General's Uniform

PART TWO: IT TAKES AN ISLAND

11. Running on Empty

12. Walk to D'Feet ALS

INVITATION

This is what Randy would say if he could…

Hello friends! What's going on? Thank you for joining me and taking time to hear my heaven on earth story. I promise I'll take it real slow as it might be a little bumpy. Strap on your belt and get a good grip. You see, my wheelchair is getting old too, and its onboard life-giving equipment makes for a heavier than normal, wall bumping, leg bruising, awkward vehicle. Oh, by the way, it won't just be a spin around the block. I'd love for you to experience a unique ride that has lasted for the better part of a quarter of a century. Almost twenty-five years! Can you imagine doing anything for that long? I can hardly believe it myself. I've been sitting in this chair almost as long as I was alive, before my confinement. *Wow: wonder what else took place during this span of time?*

Twenty-five years…

Dolly the sheep was cloned and learning to walk just about the time I began to falter. Pathfinder found its footing on Mars a couple years later. Unfortunately, our national security was shaken to the core when the World Trade Centers were tragically destroyed; and, remember the terrible Indian Ocean tsunami? On a more positive note, while we survived the non-event of the millennium bug "Y2K", most of us have embraced the technology advancements of Google, Facebook, Twitter, and more. What would we do without them now? From the literary world, we welcomed Nicolas Sparks' first love story, *The Notebook*, and from Hogwarts, only twenty years ago we met, an all grown up now, young Harry Potter. From a personal perspective, twenty-five years can be a tremendously long time.

Twenty-five years…

Or, twelve million, six hundred and fourteen thousand, four hundred minutes ….*and counting.* Some of you might realize that is approximately how many minutes I have been sitting in this chair or lying in my bed, unable to care for myself, in any way. Sad as that might sound, I am blessed to be alive and to share my treasures and God's blessings with you. While my life has taken several unanticipated turns, I have still been able to live much like the song made famous by crooner and film star Frank Sinatra's *I Did It My Way*. Perhaps you'll visit this theme while you read or if you're fortunate enough to walk down a well-traveled Emerald Isle beach path we call, *Randy's Way*.

Well, if one is going to have to sit for as long as I have without talking, moving, or even breathing without assistance, the very least one can do is have the authority and accountability to do it, …*My way*. I choose to live actively, which includes hiring and training my medical team, ensuring our house is constructed and maintained so that our family enjoys a home -- not a hospital clinic, and enjoying as normal a life as possible.

During this journey, we'll share God's grace, the power of love, importance of family and friends, and much more. Humorous anecdotes involving Marine General Officers and hippocraticly induced comments from physicians who remain amazed at my longevity will hopefully help you appreciate how much we have worked to stay alive and more importantly to help others. Ironically, some of those very doctors who thought I would die within two to five years, as is normal for ALS patients, are likely dead from old age.

ALS, Amyotrophic Lateral Sclerosis, sometimes referred to as Lou Gehrig's disease, is what provides me this unique vantage point for viewing the world from a different position. Often quickly, in less than a year, its victims ultimately die. I am one of the lucky ones in that I have beat the odds by surviving this long. But, it is not without help and pain. As you read, you'll visit with Kim, my soulmate, and I, as we fight the United States Department of Veteran Affairs, ultimately testifying before Congress, to win medical benefits for myself as well as all other similarly afflicted Gulf War Illness (GWI) veterans. Friends from childhood, college, the Marine Corps, and beautiful Emerald Isle, my island home for the past three decades, along with my loving family, will recount serious and light-hearted experiences that play a part in my being able to share with you now.

A former avid runner and combat proven Marine Corps' officer, now completely confined to my bed and/or ventilator equipped wheelchair, which I can't even control, I am eager to experience this marathon with you. While I was known for my quickness and speed, I had grown to love long runs, as I was always in it for the long haul. Similarly, from the onset of this ugly, debilitating, life-altering disease, I planned to run my longest and most successful race. In the following pages, join Kim, our two wonderful children, Nicole and Kyle, and countless friends and family members who have shared the baton in this endurance relay, proving that, "God doesn't make mistakes." Encouragingly, I have "spoken" these same words to many people who ask, "Why are you still here?" They often mean *still living,* but can't figure out a humane way to ask such a difficult question.

Although ALS robbed me of my physicality and so much more, through my hand-in-hand walk with God, I have become a better man, a more gentle and caring husband, focused family provider, conscientious patient, compassionate human being, and most importantly, a courageous Christian. Believe me, this hasn't been easy; not in the least! While the adage, "What doesn't kill you, makes you stronger" comes to mind, I prefer the proverb, "Trust in the Lord with all your heart and lean not on your understanding." I also believe in the power of people. With the help of too many to name, we offer our story and hope it will remind us that through God's Grace all things are possible.

When first diagnosed with ALS in 1995, after serving as a Marine Combat Engineer in the Gulf War, I despaired, like so many others. I watched from a distance as other war veteran experienced uncommon muscular, skeletal, and psychiatric diseases at alarming rates. Research now shows veterans who deployed to the Gulf War are two to three times more likely to get ALS as the general veteran population. *Not me, I was sure I wouldn't get sick!* Admittedly, I was aching and my hand grip was not as strong as it had been. In retrospect, I had been experiencing ALS symptoms for a while, but just didn't know it. *I was simply pushing my exercise regimen too hard.* I was sure this was an athletic injury; it just didn't seem to get any better.

The morning of my diagnosis was traumatic, to say the least. I remember telling the unfortunate physician who delivered the news something to the affect, "Doc, see this hand? I will be back in ten years to choke you with it!" *That didn't happen and I have calmed down a little bit since then, thankfully.* What I wish I had been able to say then, that comes to mind now is, "Are you threatening me with Heaven? What a beautiful gift that will be." During the writing process, this sentiment was shared with us by a beautiful young lady afflicted with a terminal disease. Her grace is perfect for how I feel.

Twenty-twenty hindsight for sure.

Once I finally accepted my diagnosis and discovered my *short* life expectancy and options, I adopted an attitude of prayer and strengthened my commitment, over time, to following God's will. In addition to helping others find God's salvation, one of my most important human missions was to immerse myself in our young children's lives and future college graduations. I have accomplished these human goals with Kim's absolute love and support and I have been able to be their dad, encouraging them to accept their spiritual Father, Jesus Christ, as their Savior.

Few of my Marine buddies would be surprised to read that I know Jesus as my Lord. However, they might be surprised to learn that I played trombone in the high school band and love most types of music. In 1970, like everyone else listening to the radio, I even sang along with a youthful Michael Jackson's, "I'll Be There." Remembering his lighthearted lyrics about, "…Bringing salvation back…," makes it even more important and meaningful to my relationship with God, my bride and children, and you!

Almost a quarter of a century later, like all of us, I continuously adjust to life's bumps and bruises – *there have been many* -- and adjust my goals. Now, I hope to witness both of our beautiful children begin their young adult lives and enter successful careers. A few grandchildren to cherish would be a nice bonus.

Everyone has their path to choose in life when facing a life altering illness. "Giving up" was certainly an option. No doubt about it, that decision crossed my mind a time or two. I chose to fight! Since I made the commitment to God and my family, I intend to win this race. I am convinced that the finish line ribbon I break will be the entrance to Heaven.

If you are still reading and I hope you are, I believe you or someone you love, may be or may have been contemplating giving up on whatever life challenges face them. I invite you to engage in our story as we capture anecdotes including the, "who, what, where, when, and how" that are central to my survival. Hopefully, our ALS story will, like a pebble in a pond, create a small ripple in health care and inspire others to fight to improve their quality of life and to search for causes and cures. It takes all of us working together to eradicate these illnesses.

All of us are also needed to help those afflicted enjoy what life they have left. I love the African proverb, "It takes a village to raise a child." Living and loving on a southern facing barrier island in eastern North Carolina, with beautiful stretches of beach that I long to run across again, I accept my lot and know that it also *takes an island,* and then some, to live and share this story. Throughout this experience, as we wrote this message about my sometime embarrassing life, I have been reminded of what the 19th century Danish theologian and philosopher Soren Kierkegaard said, "Life can only be understood backwards; but it must be lived forwards."

So, for just a little bit longer, won't you lace up your shoes and run with me?

Yours in Christ,

Randy

Author's Thoughts

I met Major Randy Hebert, pronounced "A Bear" - *we'll explain that later*, my dear friend and military hero, in a God driven way. Even now, as I pen these thoughts I'm amazed at how God purposefully led us to each other through a set of unique circumstances. Ironic or divine? I lean toward the latter. A set of unique circumstances resulted in my spending the past twelve months researching Randy's fifty-five years, looking for just the right anecdotes to help share *His* message. As I began the end of the journey, albeit the hardest part, that being sitting at a computer and physically writing the book, I was shocked by the sheer number of ironic occurrences that led us to this venture. You'll discover these later. For now, let's focus on Randy.

Recently, I thought about Randy while I enjoyed the musical, RENT, being presented at the Carteret Community Theater in Morehead City, North Carolina. Remember "525,600 Minutes" from the lyrics of the penetrating song, "Seasons of Love" famously introduced by the then socially cutting-edge Broadway musical of the same name? If you know it, you're probably humming right now; if you don't, you will be. What a beautiful message on so many levels. Reminiscing of the time I first heard it on Broadway, my mind drifted to a thought I had nearly a decade ago. A recently retired Air Force officer, I had already been diagnosed with my own life-altering illness which to this point I have shared with few people. Certainly, I am not in the same seat as Randy, literally and figuratively, and am thankful for the tremendous medical advancements and support from the Veterans Administration physicians who have allowed me to lead a somewhat normal and productive life. Nothing like the twelve million minutes Randy has been unable to move which I quickly calculated during the musical. And that number increases every single minute of every hour. *Can one imagine living with any debilitating illness over 12,000,000 minutes?*

In short, that is how long Randy has enjoyed life since being diagnosed with ALS, ironically nicknamed, "Lou Gehrig's disease" after one of the greatest professional baseball players who ever played the game. Lou Gehrig was called the "Iron Horse" due to his ability to play for such a long time and for his tremendous batting average. The Major League Hall of Famer starred as a New York Yankee ending with the honor of being the first ever to have his number officially retired. Unfortunately, like Randy, Gehrig was diagnosed at a young age when he went to the world-famous Mayo Clinic shortly after the beginning of the 1939 baseball season. Unlike Randy, Gehrig survived only two years after diagnosis and became a beacon of hope because of how he approached his illness saying, "I intend to hold on as long as possible and then if the inevitable comes, I will accept it philosophically and hope for the best. That's all we can do." Over the past nearly quarter century, Randy, Kim, Nicole, and Kyle approached this life-altering challenge with a similar spirt and the loving assistance of the entire Emerald Isle family and many, many others from around the globe. Like Gehrig, Randy and Kim remain as upbeat as possible, unknowingly also serving as a beacon, perhaps more fittingly a lighthouse, since they live on a North Carolina barrier island, for others who succumb to personal, professional, and certainly health challenges.

Like its better-known sister disease, multiple sclerosis or MS, ALS robs patients of their ability to control voluntary physical actions. Muscles begin to stiffen, *sclerosis means harden,* then get weaker and eventually decrease in size, strength, and ability. Sadly, most patients have difficulty eating, speaking, swallowing, breathing and die usually within two to five years, sometimes much sooner -- there is no known cure! While Randy is an anomaly as he has lived with ALS more than eight times longer than most patients, he is not alone. A world renown example of ALS longevity, noted theoretical physicist Stephen Hawking, has successfully lived with ALS for more than a half century. ALS for military combatants might be considered a form of being a prisoner of war. Not unlike one of my friends,

U.S. Naval Captain (Retired) Charlie Plumb, who was shot down and became a nearly six-year Vietnam POW, Randy has endured his own POW-type "locked in syndrome," with zero chance of escape.

Getting ALS is not special – living and possibly thriving with ALS is! Many people look at the diagnosis as a death sentence and eventually may "choose a different path" as Randy once told me. I didn't have the heart to ask, but I thought it meant choose to give up. I had never known anyone with ALS, although since I started writing this memoir over a year ago, it seems almost everyone knows someone who has died from or is in a fight with ALS. Remember the 2014 Ice Bucket Challenge? People across the world got engaged to share in the fight -- that is what it will take to find a cure! Interestingly, it was like this too when I began my dialysis career. Like dialysis, ALS is a non-discriminating disease. Professional athletes such as major league baseball star and North Carolina native, Jim "Catfish" Hunter, actor Sam Shepard, a former Chairman of the Joint Chief of Staff of the United States military, and even Mao Zedong, former Chairman of the Chinese Communist Party, along with people from all walks of life and countries, have been afflicted with ALS. Whomever you are, facing ALS together definitely makes it easier; but it is anything than easy. Just being able to communicate is a challenge.

Communicating with ALS is one example of how Randy role-models the unofficial Marine Corps' spirit, "Adapt and Overcome." He believes, if you can't change the situation you can at least affect the outcome. Since Randy can't talk or even turn his head in the direction of a person talking with him, it was asked numerous times, "How did he write the book?" Randy's inability to speak doesn't define his ability to think or communicate. Randy is one of the most intelligent human beings I have met. Always staring straight ahead, unless someone physically adjusts his head and shoulders, Randy communicates better than most! It just takes time.

Once his voice failed and other communication devices didn't work, Randy and his father, Loyd, developed a process they call, "ABCing." This simple system allows complete communication, even if it takes a little bit longer than what most people are used to. It works like this: To respond, make a comment, or ask a question, Randy focuses his eyes straight ahead. An attentive nurse, family member, or visitor will then quickly recite the alphabet i.e. "ABCDEF...." When Randy hears the correct letter of the first word he wants to say, he turns his eye in the direction of the person reciting the alphabet. The person will clarify the letter ensuring they have it correct, repeat the process for the second letter, and so on. Once the word is completely spelled, Randy will again turn his eye in the person's direction to indicate the word is correct. The process is repeated until the sentence, comment, or question is complete. As you think about the ease with which you just finished reading these few sentences, value how much energy it takes for Randy to share his words. I consider Randy the E. F. Hutton of ALS -- when he says something, it is meaningful and "people listen!" The bottom line is that Randy was as instrumental in the writing of this book as if he could have spoken – perhaps more so. Clearly, my visits with many people over the year gathering Randy reflections was fun, but my most enjoyable conversations were with Randy. Perhaps we might all learn from this.

Prayerfully,

Tom

Nicole age six "ABCing" with Dad

Thomas P. Gill

part one

IN THE BEGINNING

chapter one

MADE FOR THE MOVIES -- "TAKE ONE"

Running through the tree-covered undulating terrain of Fort Leonard Wood, Missouri was one of my favorite past times. The small hills of the Missouri Ozarks offer just enough challenge. To make it more intense, I simply add more miles; not unlike living at Emerald Isle, North Carolina as a young Marine when I would keep on running to make up for the flat, but visually stimulating seascape. Sometimes I would run in the sand and water to make it even more challenging – Oohrah!

Not today.

In the Spring of 1995, my Commanding Officer and our Sergeant Major decided to go for a run. We didn't have a particular route in mind and when we reached an intersection I decided to go straight instead of turning left and enduring a mile and half steep hill. I didn't know at the time that my choice, the base perimeter road, was nine miles long and sported its own steep hill. I started out fine, but wasn't mentally prepared for how my body was going to react to the run. Instead of pushing the pace, I quickly began to drag. Colonel Smith gave me grief the entire run as I struggled to stay with them.

When we crested the steep hill, we stopped for water in a nearby office.   As we started running again, my legs felt even heavier and I was soaking wet from the humidity, yet I fought to keep my knees moving.   For the first time in my life I wondered if I would make it.   There was only a half mile left but I was almost out of gas.   I didn't want to admit that ALS, which one of the doctor's suspected was my condition, was already affecting my physical body.

Shuffling onward – if I stopped I wouldn't get started again - I saw her. Just ahead, no more than a hundred yards was my beautiful bride of three years, Kim. Was this a mirage? I knew I was tired, but really – that beat?

Why would Kim be driving on this side of the fort with the kids?

Only the training schools and military ranges were over here making it an ideal place to run.

Who cares?

Thankfully, she saw me as I waved her down to pick me up. Nearly collapsing, I opened the car door and heard her say,

"Get in, I'll drive."

Although not too unusual for *my* wife, as most military men know, *that* is almost never going to happen, especially with kids in the car. But then I saw my beautiful babies, Nicole and Kyle, sitting in the back seat, and nearly crumpled.

I complied.

Kim ran the air full blast. This was painfully and obviously the last straw. I had been complaining privately, while publicly hiding my illness, for too long. What might have happened if Kim had not been there? We'll never know. In retrospect, and believe me I wouldn't have said this twenty-three years ago, but this was God's work! He placed my angel on that road.

Kim and I dated for more than three years before I was ready to settle down. A young, some say cocky -- I prefer confident, Marine living at the beach and dating a beautiful young lady – why would I want to get tied down? The daughter of a Marine Lieutenant Colonel and his bride, Kim had accompanied her parents to Hawaii for one military tour, but with her three siblings was raised in Cape Carteret, just off the island. I sure am glad they did. Not only were they great parenting role models, they also gave me a wonderful wife. Petite, pretty, with a quick-witted personality, Kim was exactly what I *hadn't* been looking for. Once again, someone was looking out for me.

We had dated on and off during several assignments that took me overseas and she was always here when I got back. Our mutual military and Cape Carteret civilian friends knew it would happen, although Kim was the one needing assured. Then, I wasn't really helping matters as I made it clear I was never getting married. What finally convinced me was my impending deployment to the imminent Gulf War. Once again, divine intervention. After I returned from the war, we married in a beautiful ceremony, followed by a reception at the Marine Corps' Camp Lejeune Officers Club, on August 15, 1992.

Just a few years later, sitting in our living quarters at Fort Leonard Wood, we were frightened and scared about the possibilities; rightfully I guess, looking back on it. Over the next few days, we talked about how my arm and grip strength had been weakening ever since leaving Emerald Isle. Admittedly, I was afraid of what I might do if I couldn't serve in the Marine Corps. Since my junior year in college, commanding Marines was all I ever wanted to do – taking charge and protecting our country. *Was that about to change? Was this the final scene?*

***

*"You will be amazed at how things magically fall into place when you **let go of the illusion of control**."* Maryam Hasnaa

"Again, I saw that under the sun the race is not to the swift, nor the battle to the strong, nor bread to the wise, nor riches to the intelligent, no favor to

those with knowledge, but time and chance happen to them all." Ecclesiastes 9:11

***

When Colonel Smith finished his run, he came right to my office. I am not a quitter, had never quit a run, and was scared beyond belief.

"Are you mad, Sir?" I started, with an atypical quiver in my voice.

"Hell yeah," he replied… Laughingly he added, "That you didn't pick me up too!"

I am reminded of Tom Hanks' line in the classic, Forrest Gump, "Life is like a box of chocolates, you never know what you are going to get." I sure didn't expect that reaction.

Thankfully, my war hardened boss is also a devout Christian who walks the walk and talks the talk! He cared for me, and through God's Grace, ensured Kim and I were reassigned back east to Camp Lejeune, North Carolina where we could be close to family and state of the art medical facilities.

chapter two

"YOUNG FRANKENSTEIN"

"Tigers die and leave their skins; people die and leave their *names.*"

Japanese Proverb

Did you ever see the movie, *Young Frankenstein*? If right now you are saying, "What hump?" or "Walk this way," you are of a certain generation in which actors Gene Wilder, Marty Feldman, Cloris Leachman, and of course Terri Garr brought laughter to the silver screen through their acting in the horror comedy by the same name. Throughout this outrageously funny movie, director Mel Brooks has his main character chastise people for mispronouncing his last name. In this 1974 classic, Dr. Frederick Frankenstein, the protagonist and a descendant of the original Dr. Victor Frankenstein, visits Transylvania to inherit his ancestral estate. However, he has always distanced himself from his maligned name and does not want people to associate him with the world renowned mad scientist. He insists his name is pronounced "Frunk-N-Steen". I love Mel Brooks' comedies and identify with the problem some people have when their name is mispronounced.

I was born in 1962 in the Texas town of Port Arthur and briefly lived as a toddler in Virginia until moving to and growing up in South Carolina. Even with Texas roots, I still pull for my South Carolina Gamecocks having spent four great years studying in Columbia. But with a heritage tracing its roots to the French side of eastern Texas and western Louisiana, I knew my last name should really be pronounced like the firefighter, Smokey, the "A" Bear." I detested when teachers and others mistakenly called me, "Her-Bert" and often even misspelled my last name. *How hard can it be?*

Now truthfully, in the Cajun country of Louisiana, there is a "Hee-Bert" High and my dad was always a "Hee-Bert." But just across the Sabine River, between the Texas and Louisiana border, our family name is accurately pronounced, "A-Bear." While there may have only been one Hebert family in South Carolina, there are over 6,000 families privileged to share this rich name throughout Louisiana. It's the most common French origin surname in the state. Appropriately enough, Hebert is derived from an old Germanic name that means "army" and "bright." For a future military officer, that sort of made sense.

Growing up in the early seventies, I was the oldest male child in a Roman Catholic family consisting of six kids in the small, southern, sleepy town of Taylors, South Carolina, a suburb of

Greenville, before the word "suburb" was popularized. It was a wonderful time to be a part of a large southern family. Please don't think I'm trying to imply that everything was always perfect. It wasn't. But, there were far more good things about being in a large family than not. We had a ready-made basketball team, if we ever wanted to play, and certainly there was never a dull moment. As the oldest boy, I was the Alpha male and most of the time my personality made me the alpha child. Some might even say I tried to run the entire family. I may not have shown it all the time, but I love all my siblings in different ways. My three sisters, Melinda, Michelle, and Melanie, along with brothers, David and Kevin, share intense loyalty to our parents and the entire family, even if we didn't always share the same affection for each other. Large families are often, by definition, dysfunctional, and certainly those familiar with recently deceased South Carolina novelist Pat Conroy will acknowledge that in his controversial works such as, *The Great Santini* and *The Prince of Tides*, families may have had difficulties displaying it, but they love each other deeply. During those hot summer months as the late sixties marched into the seventies, in the hard-scrabble red clay of rural South Carolina, we shared what is called family.

Throughout our neighborhood and the region in what South Carolinians refer to as *The*

Upstate there were kudzu covered trees flowing across rolling hills with countless opportunities for kids to play outside all day until the dinner bell rang. Not much has changed other than kids must be kept more on a leash; but then that is true in most towns and cities across the states. During this deliciously free youthful time, I was Randy Hebert, pronounced just like it looks "Hee-Bert." Sometimes it was spelled and even carelessly mispronounced "HER-BERT." As I grew up, this thoughtlessness continued to irritate me. As a Boy Scout, my buddies nicknamed me "Hebe-Jebe" because I was lightning fast and never stayed still. Eventually it was shortened to "Hebe" and in college revised to "Heebs." All of these names were fun but were predicated on the pronunciation of Hebert with a long "e" sound. That just didn't sound right. And on the global stage, even actors and news reporters mispronounce our last name. George Costanza, during one famous Seinfeld episode, tried in vain to get his friend, Julie, to correctly pronounce Bobby Hebert's, the then Atlanta Falcons quarterback, name. Another famous Hebert is confederate General Louis Hebert, who was born in Iberville Parish, Louisiana in 1820, graduated from West Point, and became a successful commander during the Civil War Battle of Vicksburg. Interestingly, General Hebert also commanded the heavy artillery units surrounding confederate stronghold Fort Fisher just a short drive from our Emerald Isle home.

An unrelated fact humorously supporting my expectation that people correctly pronounce our last name is that when I could, I loved to run and tan, with as little clothes on as possible. Laying out on top of college dorms in the winter with almost nothing on; jogging across Pebble Beach, North Carolina as a young Marine officer in then popular *short* running shorts sans t-shirt; or even today, sitting in my wheelchair soaking up the sun's rays at the beach, I love to roll up my swim suit – not as far as I might have thirty years ago - to get an all-over tan. With a predisposition to not wear clothes, how could my name not be pronounced "*A BARE?*" Totally aware of my heritage and not desiring to continuously correct friends, certainly not military superiors, I purposefully changed the pronunciation to how you know it today. Some of my siblings changed quickly. Eventually, I even won over my dad. Proof enough is his South Carolina car license tag which bears the word, "A-Bear 1." In time, all the South Carolina clan adopted the correct French pronunciation, give or take a southern accent or two.

Now, the military didn't necessarily appreciate the importance of how to pronounce my last name. *Randy's Way* was just not that important once I left my house, I guess.

Well, what exactly is the importance of a name? To quote fair maiden Juliet Capulet of the

Shakespeare play, *Romeo and Juliet*, "That which we call a rose, by any other name would smell as sweet."

Remember my Commanding Officer on that fateful Missouri run? Colonel Smith, who throughout the next few decades would become, and still is, a permanent fixture in our lives has a short story about my name too. I definitely remember the day I met him. "Rose" and "sweet" were not in the vernacular of the day. Remember too, we are Marines. I am also not suggesting that I was a Romeo, but darn it, names are important. Perhaps if my name had been Smith it might not have been so. But to me, it was then and it still is. Even my daughter Nicole politely corrected our biographer when he mistakenly inserted an extra "r" in his initial text to her at the onset of writing this book. She did this out of concern for him but also to ensure my name is honored.

Colonel Smith, now retired, is more casually called Smitty. A tall, lanky, gregarious Kentucky born man who has never met a stranger, he served the Marine Corps as a career Combat Engineer. An extremely successful and decorated senior officer, Smitty wears his hair a bit longer now and his mustache, which he has sported for decades, continues to push the norms of Marine Corps' dress and appearance. Married over forty years, Smitty is a devout Christian and sincere Marine – "United States Marine: no better friend, no worse enemy" -- is the perfect saying to capture this military hero's dedication to his country, friends, and most of all, God!

We'll hear more about Smitty a little later, but for now let me tell you about reporting in to him as a young, confident Marine captain with a perfect physical fitness report and a nearly "walk-on-water" evaluation record. A few of my superior officers highlighted in my annual reviews that I was a "poster boy" for the Marine Corps. Humbly, I accepted this moniker and tried to live up to it daily. Because of my appearance, fitness and "get stuff done" attitude, I had the opportunity to report to and be mentored by several senior officers including as Aide-de-camp to General John Arick at Cherry Point Marine Corps Air Station. To say I was self-assured might be an understatement. Then I met Smitty, at the time Major Smith.

I remember it like yesterday. After graduating from the Army Engineer Advanced Course in Fort Leonard Wood in 1990, I was transferred to the 2nd Combat Engineer Battalion of the 2nd Marine Division. As a combat engineer, newly assigned to the command, I was "dressed to kill" in my immaculate "Alpha" uniform. Like going to work on the first day of a new civilian job, "reporting in" to one's military commanding officer is the only time you must make a lasting first impression. I was ready.

So, I thought.

"Sir, Captain Hebert reporting," I remember barking, ensuring he heard my name as, "A Bear".

Apparently, he didn't.

"Ee-bert, I don't give a shit what you call yourself and I don't care for your bleach blonde hair. We're leaving for Saudi in a few days. Get your supplies and ensure your trash is ready. You're going to work directly for me. Understand?"

"Sir, yes sir," was all I could muster. It took some time and personal fortitude to readdress my name with the boss. Over time I was able to "train" Major Smith to correctly pronounce my name.

Eventually too, I went to war with this man and will do anything for him!

So, what does having my name pronounced correctly have to do with our ALS challenge? Well, the way I see it, just like fighting Saddam to ensure democracy and human rights, you must pick your battles. I figure, if you are given a name, well, people ought to say it right. And that fight, which I picked early in life, demonstrated that fighting for what's right is just about the most important thing in life. Now, fighting to ensure my fellow military members, some who gave their all, and their families receive medical care, compensation, and other veteran benefits due to them is my purpose – what could be more important?

***

Maxim 16: "Y*our name is in the mouth of others: be sure it has teeth.***"**

Howard Tayler

Colonel Smith "Smitty" and Randy during an island ALS Walk

chapter three

MY D-DAY

"For even the Son of Man came not to be served but to serve, and to give his life as a ransom for many."

Mark 10:45 (NIV)

Friday, December 21, 1990 will always be my personal *D-Day*. On that day, my Marine Division deployed to Saudi Arabia for what would begin the end of my career, and other than marriage to Kim, my life's defining moment. As painful as this might be, I want to share through this and subsequent chapters exactly what happened while we were preparing to fight the terroristic Iraqi leader, Saddam Hussein. Remember, like Hitler before him, Saddam had ordered the invasion of a neighboring country, in this case Kuwait, not believing a world coalition would intervene. We did!

It is well documented that Iraq was accusing Kuwait of stealing petroleum through what was called slant drilling under the border; in other words, illegally drilling at a slant to tap into Iraqi oil fields miles and miles away. Perhaps Kuwait was. Whatever the motivation, Saddam invaded Kuwait using about a tenth of his massive million-man army. Kuwait surrendered after a short two-day struggle while Saddam's terrorists ran rampant for the next seven months. The United Nations' allied forces eventually gave Saddam an ultimatum to leave Kuwait, which he failed to meet, necessitating the first Gulf War. This is what led to my being in Kuwait in the winter of 1991.

After "working up," or getting prepared for the impending deployment, we shipped out. Arriving in Saudi Arabia after a sixteen-hour flight from Cherry Point Marine Corps Air Station, we immediately began the back-breaking work we had trained for. Combat engineers, like their Navy Seabees and Air Force Red Horse squadron brothers, are responsible for completing construction projects allowing primary combatants to achieve their objectives. While we had many collateral responsibilities, one of our primary goals was to prepare roads for casualty evacuation using heavy earth moving equipment. I also served as Officer-in-Charge of breaching the division's left flank. Our well-trained and motivated engineers completed multiple drills, improved roadways for use by the thirty-five country coalition forces, and fortified buildings and bunkers until the war kicked off on January 17, 1991. Previously referred to as Operation Desert Shield, the invasion, now called Operation Desert Storm, lasted just one month, one week and four days ending with the expulsion of Iraq from Kuwait. The actual ground war lasted a mere one hundred hours, or as I think about time, *six thousand minutes*, until Iraq surrendered. Commanding 750,000 international forces, six-foot and three inches tall, "Stormin Norman" as General Herbert Norman Schwarzkopf, Jr., also called "The Bear" was known, routed the Iraqi defenses. The blitzkrieg type of Gulf War campaign had many positive strategic results including the reestablishment of the Kuwaiti monarchy and establishment of United Nations sanctions against Iraq.

For a while, the world was a safer place.

So, I thought. Little did I know my personal battle for survival had just begun.

My tactical actions during the war have been well documented in other sources including my congressional testimony and like others may have been caused by what is referred to as the "fog of war." Poor communications likely resulted in actions causing needless exposure to toxic chemicals known now to cause neurological diseases such as ALS. Sometimes it just takes a downstream trigger to allow this sleeping monster to awaken. Regardless, the result of actions during the war left many veterans from all coalition countries with long term chronic and/or terminal illnesses. Often, we wrongly think it is only the American veterans who suffer. There are veterans from all services, officers and enlisted members, pilots and ground pounders, combatants and non-combatants, from around the world, including women, afflicted with Gulf War syndrome diseases with symptoms including fatigue, muscle pain, memory loss, diarrhea, and chronic multi-symptom illnesses with serious consequences. Succinctly, of the nearly three quarters of a million American veterans who fought in the Gulf War, approximately thirty-seven percent suffer multiple long term chronic health concerns. A much smaller number, but of extreme importance, are veterans afflicted with ALS.

Unfortunately, I find myself in the latter group. Perhaps I may have been predisposed to having ALS – one never knows. But what I wasn't predisposed to was encountering toxic nerve agents that had been stockpiled by the Iraqis for use against coalition forces and even their own people.

The day began like every other day, even though emotions were on overdrive as we knew what was about to happen. Having been "in country" for weeks, our Marines were ready to get on with it. *The sooner we could win this war the sooner we would be headed home.* Don't misunderstand, Marines are always ready for any challenge. We prefer to not; but, if we must, we will fight and win! But the constant never-ending sand and extreme temperature changes from 115-degree afternoon sun to the evening chill as we vigilantly scanned the dark Saudi Arabian desert was beginning to take a toll. Throughout the day, if I wasn't talking with Marines while crouching in a foxhole, I was sitting in my jeep with my driver, Sergeant Frances, or conferring with my radioman, Lance Corporal Scharffbilling. We had planned, were pumped, and ready. However, serious concerns for my men raced through my mind.

To understand what was on the line and what was really going to happen one needs to understand a few things most people would usually have no need to know. First, we believed just a few miles away there were chemical and biological agents, or poisons, that Saddam would use on his own people, much less his enemy. These were stockpiled across the battlefield and dangerously close to our location. My team was in harm's way.

Randy in the desert

To protect against these invisible toxins, such as the Sarin nerve agent and Cyclosporine mixes, notwithstanding the massive choking oil fields which had purposefully been set on fire by the Iraqis, military combatants were equipped and prepared to don (wear) five levels of MOPP or Mission Oriented Protective Posture gear. The severity of impending and or known release of chemical biological attack dictated what level of MOPP gear to wear, from Zero which is least severe to Four which means complete body and breathing protection. On any given day we had our gear close at hand, were well trained, and ready to don. Donning this equipment, consisting of an overgarment, mask and hood, field gear, footwear covers, and gloves is cumbersome, but we practiced often as we believed in our lifesaving equipment. We pulled all the drawstrings to lessen the possibility of contaminants entering any opening. The order to wear specific MOPP gear is given when the highest degree of chemical or biological protection is necessary or the toxins are known to be present but the actual hazard not identified. To picture what this looks like, visualize a Marine holding his weapons and supplies and when notified hurriedly putting on additional protection; more than a fully loaded fireman rushing into a burning building. The protective gear I donned during the incident which led to at least one exposure resulting in my illness was the highest level or MOPP Four.

For several weeks, the allied coalition's nearly 2,500 combat aircraft manhandled Saddam's 500 planes softening up the battle field, destroying much of the command and control infrastructure, and decimating the morale of the Iraqi military. Low flying jet fighters screamed over our positions dropping 88,500 tons of bombs until the order for the ground war was given. Cruise missiles from our warships supported the F-14, F-15, F-16, and F/A-18 fighter bombers using laser-guided bombs. As a Marine officer, I always valued our brethren military members supporting US, but for those few weeks, I paid them the greatest respect. What they were doing through air superiority was making our job that much easier. Watching this display of military might being used for the right reason was awesome.

Finally, on Sunday, February 24, 1991 the invasion and liberation of Kuwait began. Remember, only 100 hours or *6,000 minutes* later and it was over. In those few hours my life changed, forever.

Through the clouded lenses of my memory as I relived wearing my MOPP4 gear I shared the following story with congressional leaders several years later. Many others have offered similar testimonies.

"… On 23 February 1991, the eve prior to our ground attack, we moved into our attack position approximately two and one-half to three miles from the border of Kuwait, near the area known as the elbow (Umm Gudair Oil Fields). On G-day, 24 February 1991, we were to link up with a section of tanks, this never happened. In the confusion, I radioed to the Battalion Three to let him know the situation. I decided to halt my men south of the berm dividing Saudi Arabia and Kuwait. I proceeded about five hundred meters to the east via a HUMV with my driver and radio man to a traffic control point.

As we approached, we received hand and arm signals for a chemical attack. We put on our masks and gloves. In doing so, I recall my right hand feeling cool and tingling. I was mad because

we were just starting and already receiving the sign
for chemicals. I jumped from the vehicle and
asked the Marine MP in strong Marine Corps
language who had told him to go to MOPP Level
Four. He pointed to another Marine who I asked
the same question. He told me, "Someone on the
radio."

We drove back and radioed to my Marines
to get to MOPP Level Four. When we arrived
some were, others were not. The driver and I
jumped from the vehicle giving the sign for
chemicals. I approached the MP controlling traffic
to ask why he wasn't in MOPP Level Four. He
told me the alarm was false. I was angry and
removed my mask. **I now feel that was a
mistake**. I radioed the Battalion Three and told
him, "We are rolling and we have not made
contact with the tanks."

He said, "Okay." Within a minute of rolling
he called back saying that, "Your lane is dirty,
chemical mine has gone off, go to MOPP Four."

I called back and verified his statement.
Then I told him, "Roger that." We all went to
MOPP Four. Lane Red One was the lane where
the chemical mine was detonated.

After about thirty minutes, we had finished
firing line charges. We had several mines that
needed to be cleared from the hedge row. We
were still in MOPP Four and I radioed to the

Battalion Three asking where we would decontaminate. A Lieutenant told me that we should check to see if chemicals were in the air. I again asked where we would decontaminate. I received the same response. I was mad and hung up.

We stayed in MOPP Four another two and one-half to three hours. During this time, much of the Division moved quickly through the area, some in MOPP Four, others not. Although we had finished our portion of the lane, we remained by Lane Red One because the far, right flank was having difficulty due to the density of the minefield. The Battalion Commander wanted us to proceed to the next obstacle belt together. I remember a dead camel lying by the entrance to our lane. It did not have any insects feeding on it (suggesting it had just recently been killed perhaps by poisonous gasses).

After several hours in MOPP Four, I had my driver check the area for chemicals. After we determined that chemicals were no longer present, my driver selectively unmasked. Then, after he displayed no symptoms, I had my Marines unmask. I forgot to mention that once we arrived at the breach site, I had communicated directly with the Lieutenant working with me, asking if he felt funny or if he was having trouble breathing. He told me he didn't think so but asked why. I told him I felt funny. I also recall two large explosions while we were breaching that I thought were artillery. However, they only left dust clouds after they hit. I now believe they may have been chemical rounds.

We remained between these two minefields the night of 24 February 1991 and the next night, 25 February 1991. One the 25th, I heard a large explosion in the rear area. The following day we moved to an area known as the Ice Cube Tray where we built a POW camp. I later learned the area just north was the headquarters for the Iraqi Chemical Brigade. During our movement to this area we heard several explosions. I am not sure what they were.

A few days later, 28 February 1991, we moved to an area about eight miles southwest of Kuwait City, near Al Jahra. I later learned this area was an old garbage dump that had been covered. Around the beginning of March, perhaps the tenth, I became very ill with flu like symptoms. I remember many others were ill also.

Around the 22nd of February, I started taking the Pyridostigmine Bromide (PB) Pills for anti-nerve agent protection. I believe I took the pills for eleven to fourteen days. Once we returned to Saudi Arabia in early April, I began to have some difficulty with sleep. This continued upon my return home on 15 May 1991 until early July, at which time I was having difficulty reading and remembering what I had read. I was extremely aggressive, moody, and excitable. I had headaches, vomiting, and diarrhea. I was also diagnosed with moderate depression. I was given medications for several months, at which time the majority of the symptoms went away.

I continued to have headaches almost on a daily basis and took as many as eight to ten aspirins a day until April 1995. Besides the headaches, I felt I was not able to breathe as well when I ran. In May of 1994 I noticed a decrease in my upper body strength. In early July, I had a lump on my throat area the size of a walnut. I was not sick. I had a friend, who is a medical doctor, come to my home to examine me. He was not sure what caused the lump. It remained for one and a half to two weeks.

In October of 1994, I experienced problems with my throat muscles and coughed very frequently and uncontrollably. There were times when my throat muscles would constrict and I could not breathe for ten to fifteen seconds. In November of the same year, I noticed atrophy in my right arm and hand and began having difficulty controlling my hand and arm.

In January 1995, while being evaluated at the National Naval Medical Center, I developed another lump on the right side of my face just forward of my right ear. It also was the size of a walnut. During the same three-week period, I had a very large rash from the middle of my nose to the middle of my forehead which was red, swollen, and extremely itchy. Also, it had three white watery pustules. When the rash subsided, I was left with a scar between my eyebrows.

From January 1995 until October 1995 I was evaluated at several different hospitals. During some of these visits, I saw, spoke to, and learned of other service men and women who served in the Gulf who were having problems. These problems included cancer, respiratory disease, muscle twitches, fatigue, memory loss, joint pains, ulcers, rashes, lumps under the skin, hearing problems, atrophy of one limb (Monomelic Amyotrophy – a rare disease in the United States), atrophy of the brain, insomnia, depression, heart problems, tearing of the eyes, and others.

During this time, I developed a rash on my buttocks, tearing of the eyes with burning, and occasional ringing in both ears. In October 1995 I was diagnosed with ALS (Amyotrophic Lateral Sclerosis also known as Lou Gehrig's Disease). **I believe the medical problems I have discussed are due to low level chemical exposure over an extended period.**

I learned after the war that the chemical mine detonated in Lane Red One was confirmed for the nerve agent Sarin and also the agent

Lewisite Mustard Gas by a FOX vehicle (chemical, biological, radiological and nuclear or CBRN reconnaissance vehicle) in the lane. I also learned that two Marines in an Amtrack received chemical burns and that the chemical mine confirmation was reported by the Regimental Commander of the Sixth Marines. It was also reported up the chain of command by the Second Marine Division Commander. It has been brought to my attention that there have been at least seven other cases of ALS in service members who served in the Gulf (Many more since this was originally presented in 1996). To me this is more than a mere chance or coincidence.

...Finally, on 12 November 1996 the Commandant of the Marine Corps was speaking at Camp Lejeune (where I was then assigned). I had an opportunity to ask him if the Marine Corps had an official position on Gulf War Syndrome/illness. The Commandant told me that the Marine Corps does have a position and that they believe chemical weapons were used. He also said the Marine Corps is in the process of trying to contact Marines who may have been exposed.

My favorite question is, "So what?" In other words, telling war stories and aftereffects is important, but what will we do with this knowledge? This is the central issue.

In a recent VA update, there are suggestions that as many as 200,000 American service members have been afflicted by the symptoms discussed earlier. While the exact number of Gulf War veterans afflicted with ALS may never be known, the percentage is certainly much higher than found in the average American population.

Having the opportunity to share my testimony with Congress and now, twenty years later, you, allows me to further illustrate the importance of everyone knowing the atrocity that was Saddam Hussein. We must never let this happen again. There are countless victims throughout the world that need a strong United States and allied coalition to help them enjoy the life that God expects us to have. And, we need to protect our own military forces before, during, and after conflicts.

Surviving the horror of war; the dead camels, toxic burning oil fields, and bloating enemy bodies littering the desert, and now, living with ALS, while trying to provide a *normal* life for my family, is our opportunity to demonstrate, "With God, all things are possible." In the words of the great American President Theodore Roosevelt, "Do what you can with what you have where you are." That's all I'm trying to do. In the Marine Corps, we have a saying that embodies our core values of Honor, Courage and Commitment. Any man or woman who has earned the Marine

Corp's Eagle, Globe and Anchor will realize Kim
and I are simply putting into practice this
unofficial Marine Corps slogan, "Improvise, adapt
and overcome."

chapter four

"ALWAYS DO RIGHT-THIS WILL GRATIFY SOME AND ASTONISH THE REST"

Mark Twain

I'll give Randy a break as he has shared the past ten thousand words with you. When one can talk or write, that is not too difficult. Try telling or writing a story when you can do neither. After spending more than a year talking with Randy, friends and family, I am still woefully inept at knowing how he and Kim have accepted this challenge with such grace. *Bear* with me as I work to weave the spirit and wonder of their journey into the following pages.

In the early days, Randy was known for antics such as going out on his front porch early every morning, throwing back his shoulder length bleach-blond hair, and yelling through his sleepy South Carolina tree covered neighborhood, "What's Going Onnnn?" Were you able to picture radio and television comedian Robin Williams in the 1988 movie, *Good Morning Vietnam*? Nearly forty years later, a close friend describes Randy as still always wanting to know, "What's going on?" at parties, on the beach, in large and small groups; basically, wherever he is. He should know, as he has been a friend since Randy was a young Marine

Corps officer. *Curious observer of life* might be another way to describe his intense desire to know everything. Interestingly, the friend was unaware of Randy's childhood trademark. Even today, as I reflect on my chats with Randy, he always asks about my family and "What's going on?"

Before Randy was confined to a wheelchair, quite bluntly, he was a stud. He was the kind of guy other guys wanted to be around – because girls would be nearby. It's still true today. His always impeccable dress and well-manicured hair, wiry six-foot tall runner's body, and impressive ability to talk with anybody; well, Randy was somebody you wanted to be seen with. While attending The University of South Carolina, Randy was Forrest Gump, before the movie came out -- he literally ran everywhere. In tight blue jeans or shorts, tennis shoes or topsiders, Randy was a running fool. His thin waist and broad shoulders showed it. He carried this superior physique into the Marine Corps where he always scored in the top of his class during annual fitness tests. But he wasn't always a stud. As pictures show, although Randy loved to primp and flex his muscles, until he got to high school, he was of average proportion. He might have even been a bit of a misfit as a young teenager.

One of my favorite sports stories is about Randy being on what was lovingly referred to as the Taylors, SC area "Bad News Bears." As a junior high school age baseball player, Randy was picked to be on this team which unexpectedly went on to win their league championship. Truth be told, it was a handful of rejects from all the other area teams. What Randy and others recounted is that their coach took this mismatched group of teenage baseball "rejects" and molded them into a successful winning baseball team. Coach Chip Beardsley, barely nineteen and only slightly older than his players, instilled discipline, camaraderie, and most of all, hope, into those eighteen young boys, giving them all a taste of snatching triumph from despair. Randy would remember these lessons and put them into action the rest of his life.

And like most of us, Randy wasn't always the most obedient pre-teenager. Loyd and Shirdale, Randy's parents who still live in the family home, shared how one day a man came to the home complaining about Randy throwing rocks at his car. As you'll remember, Loyd is the father of six kids, ranging from thirteen to two years old in a time when corporal punishment was in vogue. If you got punished by your parents, you might even get smacked from the neighbor's mom -- it seemed that every neighbor's mother was always watching. Well, in this circumstance, Loyd yelled for Randy to come down to the living room to which he sped, in his white superman underwear. He didn't want to make his dad wait. Well, when Loyd asked Randy if he had thrown "rocks" at this man's car, Randy said, "no." Upon closer scrutiny, when Loyd asked if he had thrown "A" rock and hit the man's car, Randy admitted to the crime. Found guilty, Loyd made Randy apologize and guaranteed that Randy would pay for the damages which amounted to $1.97. The message Randy learned from this experience was to always tell the truth and to not quibble with facts. As a young Marine commander this experience would come back to serve him well.

In early 1993, Randy oversaw a Marine company preparing to go to Haiti to help ensure peace in light of the impending coup. As related by now retired Marine Sergeant Major Gary Daniel, "Randy was a driven young officer. It was amazing how much his Marines loved and respected Randy. It is not usually this way but they seemed to know he cared. In fact, I was sort of jealous of Randy—he had just as tight of connection with the enlisted Marines as I did – they loved him. He visited regularly in their barracks checking on them at night and even bought the enlisted men a rug for the game room out of his own pocket. It would have taken too long to get it through normal channels."

"Gary," I asked, "Can you tell me why they admired Randy?"

"Absolutely. Let me give you an example. Bravo company of the 8th Engineer Support

Battalion stationed in Camp Lejeune was preparing for a short notice temporary deployment to repair roads and infrastructure while also demonstrating a show of force in Haiti. There was rioting and killing of people – it was crazy and chaotic. About 1900 hours (7:00 pm), we were told to get ready to deploy, but all of our Marines' rifles would have to be locked in what is called the cruise box."

"So, what happened?"

"Randy was in the recreation room when he heard that only officers and staff noncommissioned officers would be allowed to carry sidearms. He was livid."

With tears forming in his eyes, Randy said, "I am going to tell the Colonel I will resign my commission. We can't allow our Marines to go into harm's way without protection."

"He meant it!"

"And?"

"Lo and behold, the Marine Corps cancelled our deployment but not before the Marines had heard about what Captain Hebert was going to do. That is the reason when he was transferring to another position out of the company the men gave Captain Hebert a 'roar at the top of their lungs' to say goodbye." *This is extremely unusual for an officer to get such a resounding send-off.*

Sergeant Major Daniel and Randy

Another ironic story Sergeant Major Daniel reminisced about is Randy being an "Animal in the Marine fitness test."

"One time, when I was the First Sergeant, three senior members of the staff were joking about Randy's PFT getting a little weak – it wasn't and Gunny Hollingshed begged them to be quiet as he did not want to pay the price for Randy proving his fitness." In fact, they did another time on the Camp Lejeune main service road where many Marine companies go on forced marches.

"As the senior enlisted member, I was in front and leading at a good pace. I was six feet tall and one hundred and seventy pounds and a strong runner. Randy and I were side by side when, without speaking, we challenged each other and continued to push the pace. We kept pushing each other without concern for our Marines. Eventually we looked back and saw physically fit exhausted Marines trying to keep up. When we gathered the troops we both apologized which is almost unheard of from a First Sergeant and definitely from the commander. This and other acts of empathy endeared Randy to his Marines!"

Marines on a Hump

"Service to others is the rent you pay to live on Earth."

Muhammad Ali

chapter five

FAMILY JEWELS

"Help your brother's boat across, and your own will reach the shore."

Hindu Proverb

Certainly, by percentage, large families have expectations for more good things to happen than in smaller families. But then, the opposite applies too. And, well, the Hebert family has seen their share of tragedies and hardship. After Randy was stricken with ALS, his brothers, sisters, parents, and the extended Hebert clan, from South Carolina to Texas, surrounded him with love and support. Coupled with the love of Kim's large family in North Carolina they moved into the *new normal* of managing family gatherings around the Emerald Isle calendar.

During this time tragedy struck several times without warning. Randy's father-in-law, retired Lieutenant Colonel Sanford, also a fitness stud, died unexpectedly after working nearly non-stop boarding up their house and his in preparation for the devastating Hurricane Isabel which made landfall on the North Carolina Outer Banks on September 18, 2003. Kim's mom was tragically killed in a nearby car accident just a few short years later. These were huge burdens to place on the young family as they continued their struggle with raising two children and a dad with ALS. A fire that destroyed a large part of their home added fuel for a family disaster. Finally, Randy's little sister, Michelle, was diagnosed with triple negative invasive ductal carcinoma stage three breast cancer right before Christmas in 2010. At this point Randy had already been living with ALS for over fifteen years. *How much more could a family endure? What would this do to Randy's desire to live?*

The primary difference between the Hebert family and other families who also encounter personal challenges is summarized in one sentence Dr. Phil said on a recent talk show, "Winners do what losers won't." The Hebert family is full of fighters and winners!

In March 2014, just a few months before youngest sister Michelle passed away, Melanie was visiting the South Carolina family home. Randy's mom, Shirdale, had suffered a mini stroke and "slight" heart attack. Melanie was staying there along with Michelle to help. One evening as they sat around the dining room table eating dinner Michelle looked at the others and said, "We all know we are going to die at some point - but just because they told me I am supposed to die before each of you - doesn't mean I am supposed to quit living, am I? Imagine if Randy would have quit living because he knew he was supposed to die within three years of his diagnosis!" Melanie recounted how Randy always inspired Michelle to fight! Sure, the past two decades have been challenging, but there have also been fun and humorous events that help seal the family bond.

Take for example the boys road trip to Texas. Allow me to set the stage. Picture three grown sons including Randy in his wheelchair and their dad crammed into Randy's van loaded with medically necessary equipment and supplies departing on a twelve-hundred-mile drive to their hometown of Port Arthur, Texas. Like Pat Conroy's southern Marine Meechum family in *The Great Santini,* some of the Hebert family members were anxious about the trip but all knew they had to take one trip home for Randy.

In retelling this most memorable male bonding adventure, youngest brother David and his wife Nicola, laughed as they remembered perhaps the most precious of their learning experiences. They shared how Randy had always been obsessed with his grooming, especially his hair. ALS didn't change this. Well, after the cramped two-day drive to Texas the four guys checked into a nearby hotel to rest before seeing Melinda and the rest of the Texans. The following morning each quickly proceeded to ready themselves and collectively prepared to assist Randy. Unfortunately, the hotel did not have a handicap accessible room available and like the Hebert winners they are, they improvised. A vintage, folding, webbed, vinyl deck chair became their makeshift handicap shower seat.

What the brothers didn't realize is how hot Randy likes his showers and how insanely long he wants to take them to ensure he is clean. Plus, it feels good. *If one is sitting all day at least one can start out feeling good.* Next, David and Kevin discovered how particular Randy remains about his hair grooming. After washing his hair several times and drying it, Randy then took three times longer than any normal man should to comb his hair -- it had to be perfect just like in high school. Once again, if you can reach up and do it yourself it probably isn't that big of a deal.

The final straw, while Melinda waited for her bothers and dad for three hours, is when Randy asked his brothers to adjust his "family jewels." Remember, Randy had already lost the use of his arms. Middle brother Kevin said it succinctly for all men present and those reading now, "Randy, we aren't Kim or a nurse. We'll only adjust your balls one time!" While most families will do nearly anything for each other, Hebert male bonding, just like in most other families, apparently has a threshold that will not be crossed.

All kids may not be equal in intellect, physique, or other attributes, but the adage, "blood is thicker than water," is time and time again proven true as Randy, the alpha male, serves as a role model for his brothers and sisters. Randy's love for his siblings surpasses Cersei Lannister, Queen Regent of the Seven Kingdoms, in the world-wide popular television series and novel by the same name, Game of Thrones. Borrowing from their Texas roots, one suspects the Hebert kids invoked the unspoken code of, "Don't Mess with Heberts," which is true in many families. Even Queen Cersei is unable to bring herself to have her bodyguard squash her impish brother, Tyrion, who constantly thwarts her reign. However, that doesn't mean Randy and the other kids, normally within the chronological construct, won't take advantage of each other.

Road Trip Gang and sister, Melinda: Jan 1998

One sibling, sometimes mistaken for Randy's twin sister, is Melanie. Just one-year younger, she is a current-day example of how Randy might appear without ALS. "Mel" is a tall, slender, athletic, gregarious, energizer-bunny kind of woman, seemingly without an "off" button, and of course, very, very tanned. On family vacations, Melanie and Randy would race to be "first to the beach" and would always be the last ones back at the end of the day. Even then, tanning was a critical function of their competitions. Years ago, during one family beach trip, Mom and the kids were at a convenience store shopping for Coppertone suntan lotion. According to Mel, "Even Mom knew how important tanning was as she told the helpful clerk, 'Oh, no, no no! This one has sunscreen – we want the one WITHOUT sunscreen.'"

Talking with Melanie allows those who had not had the opportunity to know Randy in his earlier years a glimpse into what he might have sounded and looked like then and now. Like all the kids, Melanie loves Randy and mourns the progression of the disease that robbed them of their big brother. But that doesn't keep her from remembering when he was simply the alpha male oldest brother.

With mixed emotions Melanie shared an experience when as a middle-school aged girl she returned home from a beach trip with a family friend only to find Randy wearing one of her favorite gold t-shirts. "This was the maddest I probably ever got at Randy. A girl can only have so many *favorite* t-shirts at the beach and he had literally cut it off right under the chest! That was the style, especially if you wanted to show off your washboard stomach. He couldn't have cut off one of *his* shirts! No way would he do that."

Or perhaps it was the time when they were both in high school and Melanie found him working on his VW Beatle – underneath it to be exact – lying on the ground in her favorite polo shirt. It was white with little horizontal purple stripes. "Of course, I was mad as hell while Randy looked up at me and said, 'Mel – geez, it's no big deal!!' That may be the time Mom started saying Randy's philosophy is, 'What's mine is mine and what's yours is mine.'" In all seriousness, Randy was very generous helping other siblings with college loans and offering support when needed. All the same, Randy was and continues to be, the big brother who would give you the shirt off his back – *just realize it might not even be his shirt.*

Oh, no, no, no! This one has sunscreen – we want the one WITHOUT sunscreen

Randy working on his tan

***

"I may fight with my siblings, but once you lay a finger on them you'll be facing ME."

chapter six

"I NEVER LET MY BEST FRIEND DO STUPID THINGS...ALONE"

Anonymous

Fish and Randy, Taylors, SC 1975

Keith Fisher, or Fish as Randy fondly calls him, was Randy's best friend in junior high. Interestingly, I learned quickly that it was not uncommon for everyone I spoke with to say they were Randy's "best friend." In this case, these two buddies were, "thick as thieves" as Fish remembers. June 1973 marked Fish's first encounter with Randy while eating KFC on his new back porch. Fish's family had just moved into Randy's neighborhood. Suddenly, a mane of long blonde hair flashed in his peripheral vision. Running to the front porch and then to the back porch, Fish never caught the mysterious observer checking out the new family – of course it was Randy. Eventually they became fast friends including Fish even spending the night with Randy and Kim at their beach house forty years later.

In the interim, much water passed under the proverbial bridge. But time could not dampen the memories each shared. Randy's eyes danced and Fish's laughter was infectious as we spoke about their wrecking bikes on ramps, riding trails through woods, popping wheelies to see who could ride the furthest (Fish won with 356 pedals), building their own A-frame camping tent and playing Army, sometimes with imaginary weapons, which may have been predictive of Randy's chosen profession, albeit the wrong military service. All in all, they shared a Tom Sawyer and Huckleberry Finn relationship, without the river. I delight in sharing Fish's other memories which were intriguing and likewise suggestive of who Randy was to become.

"Randy was soooo proud of his looks. He read *GQ* and would follow all the fashions. I remember when Randy was about fourteen. He had a comb crease in his back pocket and in the style of the day was always blowing his shoulder length blonde hair out of his eyes. Randy was also "borrowing" his dad's really narrow ties and would wear them as well as tuck his sweater into his pants to show off his tight butt. We roomed together for a year while attending USC and Randy constantly searched for ways to maintain his deep dark brown tan; even in the winter. During the coldest months Randy would often tan on top of the men's dorm, sometimes sheltered by the air conditioning unit, in the smallest pair of shorts he could find. But that wasn't always enough. He would often roll them up so they would be as small as a speedo which only Randy could make attractive. Randy would even occasionally saunter over to the nearby hotel swimming pool and lay down on a chaise as if he was a paying customer. The fascination, some might say obsession, with tanning continues today. Ask Randy what he wants for any special occasion such as a birthday and there is a good chance it will be suntan lotion. After all, Randy's primary job is to, "go to the beach."

Even now, when the temperature allows Randy to either head to the beach or venture out to the driveway, what Randy refers to as his "concrete beach," you'll find him with his shorts rolled up high and suntan lotion covering his body. During an early encounter this past year with a new nurse, I observed Randy trying to coax her to move the ventilator tubing from his right arm. Finally, even though new to the ABC communication process, I suggested the tube laying across his arm might be the source of Randy's anxiety. It was. The nurse quickly moved it so Randy could get an all over tan. *Who's ever heard of a ventilator tan line?*

Randy's early years with Fish and others were fun crazed and filled with courage and confidence. There wasn't anything he wouldn't try. "The Heebs absolutely wasn't afraid of dying then as proven by his fearlessly performing double gainers and flips off the high diving board – of course to impress the girls. And once I remember when Randy was playing safety on the high school football team, he charged his opponent so hard, when he hit him he was nearly knocked out. No fear!!!"

Continuing a bit more seriously Fish added, "When I last visited Randy I asked him about his fear of dying to which he responded, 'I've made my peace with God and accept my fate.' I was impressed that Randy was so mature about the situation."

At the same time Randy wasn't always mature. "While Randy never got in trouble, part of that is because he didn't get caught. He was a straight shooter but he wasn't perfect and he wouldn't say he was. One time I remember when

we were bussing tables at the local Western Family
Steakhouse. As you probably know by now,
Randy was highly competitive (he still is) and
suggested we race to buss the tables and get back
to the kitchen without dropping anything. We did
and soon afterwards as I was rinsing and Hebert
was stacking, I sprayed him with the hose for
about fifteen seconds. I'll never forget Randy's
face when the manager, Mr. Jim Medlin, came in
asking, "You boys like working here?" "Yes sir,"
came Randy's immediate and apologetic reply,
even though he was not the culprit-this time."

While Randy usually came out on top of his
escapades, there were a few times he did not.
"One of my memories precedes the modern-day
television show Shark Tank. A friend was
attacked by a bulldog named Devil. It ripped his
ear off which made Randy petrified of dogs. And,
since he used to run outside all the time we
decided to make a dog repellant by mixing all sorts
of chemicals. It must have worked as our test
subject, Apollo, the neighbor's German Shepherd,
whined and scratched furiously at his eyes after we
sprayed him with the concoction." *Wonder what
the Sharks would have thought about that?*

"My reflection of Randy is that this situation
must be very difficult for him as he was always the
most active one of the guys. Randy wouldn't even
go to a movie because he didn't want to sit down
for two hours. He was either playing a game,

riding his bike, or running in the creek. I'll always cherish being Randy's best friend because of how he treated me and valued me unconditionally."

***

"Always do right-this will gratify some and astonish the rest." Mark Twain

Randy and Fish flexing in 1975

chapter seven

BAD HAND

"Life is not always a matter of holding good cards, but sometimes, playing a poor hand well."

Jack London

A college "best friend," who would also serve in the Marine Corps, in part because of Randy, is Lieutenant Colonel John O'Brien. Humorously, Randy met John after they both returned to the USC campus following the 1983 college Christmas break. What Randy didn't know was that John had been vacationing at his parent's home in Florida.

Their first exchange, initiated by Randy, started something like, "Hey man, where'd you get that tan?" As they say in the movies, "The rest is history." They became as inseparable as Fish and Randy had been in junior high even living together at the *infamous* Emerald Isle Pebble Beach. Infamous in that Randy was always tanning, if not at Camp Lejeune or on a beach run, and all the women, young and old, were asking about him.

Best Friends in '97 - Check out the tan!

John recounted, "Randy was dealt a really bad hand, maybe the worse card hand possible, and it didn't change him -- unless it made him stronger."

Having only watched family home movies of Randy as a handsome, vibrant young man, full of character, and able to talk, this became more relevant as I journeyed through his life.

"Randy continues to demonstrate leadership and discipline from a wheelchair. With his family, friends, and even his nurses and aids, Randy ensures he is still the father in the family and all joking aside, Kim allows it. Seriously, even when Randy might be ill, if the kids were in trouble Kim would say, 'Go to your father. All he had to do

81

was look at them. But then, they would crawl into his lap to kiss him and say goodnight. He was always the good guy."

"The leadership Randy demonstrates as an ALS survivor is the same selfless devotion to friends he displayed when I was failing at the Marine Corps' Officer Candidate School." All Marine officers must complete this intense school to serve as commissioned officers. "I remember it like yesterday. I was very concerned that I would fail the course which would be a huge disappointment to my family, especially my father. Out of the blue, into my squad room walked Randy, a squared away Second Lieutenant. I politely said, "Sir, you can't be in here." I worried what my Drill Instructor might say. Randy convinced me to join him in his nearby Volkswagen where he gave me the best pep talk of my life resulting in my successful graduation, commissioning, and essentially my entire military career. Now, I get to pay back those words of inspiration, shared when I was at my lowest, to help my best friend through this challenge."

A touching example of Marine Corps brotherhood is John's reflection of Randy's military retirement ceremony. Randy, who had been being driven to work because he could not safely drive anymore, painfully struggled, with added assistance from Kim and her father, to stand at attention for the Marine Corps Hymn. "There wasn't a prouder moment in my life as I saw my good friend standing tall, bent on beating this illness. Randy was demonstrating supreme leadership to all those attending, even as he was leaving the service."

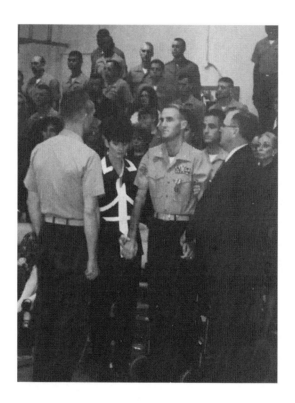

"I regularly call Randy the day after we celebrate the annual Marine Corps birthday as I know he will be inundated with more than a hundred calls and I won't get through. Randy is that kind of leader and friend. From 2002 to 2004,

I was on reserve orders and eventually activated to active duty at Camp Lejeune enabling me to visit Randy frequently. I had wondered how he would be as a father. Not surprisingly, I saw Randy rise to this challenge, too."

As he did while serving as a young captain with the Eighth Engineers, taking command of a group of unmotivated Marines, turning them into a high functioning team, and eventually winning the coveted "Commander's Cup," Randy used the same charisma and training to become a wonderful and loving father. John added, "Children don't come with a play book or directions, and they certainly don't when Dad has ALS. But, with Kim's help and Randy's desire, he fathered his kids through knee scrapes all the way to college graduation. Like his kids do today, his Marines thanked him for his loyalty and support."

Nearly one thousand of the same Eighth Engineers cemented this appreciation to Randy by actively participating in the five ALS walks that Kim and her good friend, Kelly Rogers, who lost her young husband to ALS, spear-headed on Emerald Isle helping raise over one half million dollars for ALS research.

John also shared how Kim was so strong early on handling the household basically in "survival mode" with the unexpected turn in the marriage. As we have heard from others, John admires Kim's devotion to her husband as she railed against the VA until they provided nursing assistance to care for him.

"By staying alive, Randy has made his children better human beings," and his positive nature which exuded from him in college, still shines with his nursing staff. Randy's intense training complements their formal education and ensures they understand exactly what is necessary. As he did with his Marines, before every nurse leaves, Randy thanks them for taking care of him.

Marines on ALS Walk near Pebble Beach, Emerald Isle

chapter eight

"ONE FOR ALL, AND ALL FOR ONE."

Alexandre Dumas

One of Randy's most faithful Marine Corps buddies is a man who has visited every year since Randy got sick, unless he was deployed or also ill. I caught up with Marine Lieutenant Colonel Dick Donnelly, "The Dickster," as Randy calls him, while he was completing an extended senior military officer training program in Rhode Island.

Dick has remained a constant companion embodying the Marine motto, "*Semper Fi*" or Always Faithful! His remarkable insight into Randy's psyche helped provide a perspective I had been missing. Perhaps it is because like Randy, he also has southern roots, hailing from Savannah, Georgia; is an athlete having played and coached sports at his alma mater, the United States Naval Academy; and, is a highly polished military officer. In fact, *GQ* has also been used to describe Dick.

Certainly, Randy's brash and cocky attitude and love of the Marine Corps played well to Dick. As young officers, they were inseparable and Dick loved being around Randy. "He was one of a thousand but no one was jealous of him because he never took himself too seriously. People just naturally wanted to follow him. He was the last guy in the world I thought would ever get sick. Then, when he did, we thought it would only last a few years, and here he is more than twenty years later."

In some way, The Dickster may be responsible for Randy still being alive. One night on Emerald Isle, Randy and Dick went to an island bar and saw two attractive ladies. One of them, Dale, Kim's sister, happened to be dating another Academy graduate, now retired, Navy Captain Jeff Baquer. The other was Kim. When Randy and Dick walked in; well, you've heard of love at first sight. It seems like Randy and Kim were bitten by the same bug. They became inseparable from that point on as Dick made room and the Three Musketeers were formed. Since Kim had been raised in Cape Carteret, just off the island, she had a strong social network, and both loved the beach; it was a match made in heaven.

Dale, Jeff, Kim and Randy

Dick said, "I didn't realize the strength of Kim's character until much later." Not until Randy got sick. "It takes a special kind of person to have that loyalty… to keep the wedding vows…she does it out of love." He added, "Some people would be tempted to dismiss Randy or anyone else in that condition and treat them like a piece of furniture. Not Kim. She talks about him as if he's not even sick. Together they have created a loving and normal partnership. This family is amazing to see and a role model for others who may need to work closer together to overcome obstacles. The proof is in the pudding! The kids are super loyal and are like old heads on young shoulders."

The Dickster also shared a funny anecdote about how during a visit, before Randy used his ABC method to communicate, they had been talking and asking questions for a very long time. At this time, "Randy had been using a contraption that was hooked to his knee so he could type out his responses – it was a huge pain in the ass, but that was all he had." However, while they were talking it had not been hooked up to print off his responses. When they finally "hooked" him up the answers started spilling out, five to ten at a time. "I couldn't even remember what the questions were, while Randy had been storing them in his incredible memory, like a computer, so he could eventually respond."

Dick also shared his first visit after Randy's diagnosis. "Randy was clearly going downhill. He was having trouble enunciating and walking. During the day, Randy took me by the arm and we managed to walk the quarter mile to the beach."

The Marine buddies sat on the sand and reminisced about life. Dick asked, "Heebs, remember when we would throw the football on the beach?" Randy simply replied, "We'll throw the football again one day."

It didn't dawn on The Dickster until he was driving back to Atlanta that Randy was talking about throwing the ball later as a born-again Christian. "Randy has never publicly displayed any bitterness or feeling sorry for himself. He believes this is simply a transitory state. Randy was destined to serve his country and well, things happen during war."

chapter nine

WILD MAN

"If you obey all the rules you miss all the fun."

Katherine Hepburn

Would it surprise you to learn that Keith Meacham, a southern gentleman and lawyer, although these terms are not always used in the same sentence, from Greenville, South Carolina, was Randy's "Best Friend," lived in the same college dorm, and was very aware of the need for Randy to keep a great tan? I didn't think so. Perhaps we'll share another side of Randy now that we have *exposed* these sides sufficiently. Keith's vivid memories of living with Randy document that while Randy was a fine student he also had a bit of a wild side. Some might call him a little crazy but Keith remembers a college student high on life and what we might have called a "hell raiser."

Randy was, "One speed, wide damn open, doing his World Wrestling Federation champion Ric Flair holler, everywhere he would go." Remember Seinfeld? Randy's intro was something akin to Kramer's sliding intro into every room.

As Keith described a slightly different Randy than others shared, I got the sense that this description was more like he was in junior high, just older.

"Randy was always high on life; you know, the kind of guy who never met a stranger. Nothing's changed since then. Tom, let me tell you about Randy tanning."

Interrupting, I said, "It's okay Keith, I've heard about how important that is to him."

"Not this one."

"Okay, I'm interested," I replied.

"In early 1980 I went looking for Randy; needed to talk to him about something; don't remember what. Anyway, I knew he would probably be up on the dorm roof, tanning. He was. This time, Randy had found the most secluded place and had taken everything off, except one sock. And, well, the sock wasn't exactly on his foot. You can take it from there. Just know Randy wasn't going to have a tan line this year."

"Yep, Keith, You're right. I had not heard that story." By now, not much surprised me.

Keith remembered another anecdote aptly capturing Randy's wild man spirit. "Remember talking about wrestler Ric Flair?"

"Sure."

"Well one time, the gang decided to paper Randy into his dorm room by taping sheets of paper across his doorway while he slept. Randy woke up a little early; we were just about finished. When he opened his door, he saw our nearly completed work and knew what we were up to. Before we knew what was happening, Randy stepped back and with the carelessness of a football player raced toward the paper covering his doorway."

If we had only moved the table we had been standing on.

"Randy hit the table, caromed violently off the wall, and fell to the floor. After lying dazed on the dorm floor for what seemed like minutes he jumped up, threw back his head, gave his *Ric Flair holler*, and laughed about the whole episode. That was Randy!"

"Another time, when Randy had to take the biggest, nastiest, green sofa I've ever seen back home from college he borrowed his mom's seven passenger gold station wagon. As we loaded the sofa I noticed the front tire needed air."

"Not a problem," Randy said. He was ready to get home.

"It took about ten minutes to drive off the USC campus and as soon as we hit Interstate 26 Randy buried the needle. It wasn't even a two-hour drive home and Randy was driving at breakneck speed--in excess of 120 miles per hour. We arrived alive but after that terrifying ride I swore I would never get in a car with him again, and I didn't. That's Randy, only one speed, full steam ahead."

chapter ten

THE GENERAL'S UNIFORM

"Fall seven times, get up eight."

Japanese proverb

Just as Keith Meacham related Randy was nearly always perfect, retired Marine Corps Brigadier General John Arick and his wife, Terry, also shared fond memories of when Randy was perfect and one memory when Randy absolutely made what he considered a huge mistake. In the mid to late 80's, Randy was already demonstrating to senior leadership that he was a young officer to watch. "Lots of potential; poster boy for the Marine Corps; outstanding fitness and grooming standards…" were common comments made about Randy. These kudos led to Randy's selection to serve as the Aide-de-camp for one of the senior leaders of the 2nd Marine Air Wing (MAW) at Marine Corps Air Station, Cherry Point in nearby Havelock, North Carolina.

General Arick and Terry continue, now almost thirty years later, to stay in touch with Randy and consider the Heberts part of their family. This is primarily because of the important role Randy played in the General's success as leader of thousands of Marines responsible for operating hundreds of aircraft at multiple locations. It was a huge job with an awesome responsibility. "Aide-de-camp," like Hebert, is of European origin and means, "A subordinate military or naval officer acting as a confidential assistant to a superior, usually to a general officer or admiral." Hence, Randy knew what was going on at the highest levels of the 2nd MAW while at the same time his responsibilities included helping the General handle less complicated duties so he could focus on more challenging issues. No one could have been better prepared than Randy at ensuring the General was on time, in the right uniform, and at the right place with all of the background information required for the event -- except for an isolated incident, which to this day Randy continues to characterize as the day he slipped up.

General Arick considered Randy to be a superior professional with exceptional situational awareness; and, while not a requirement for the job, Terry added, "He's charming too." But on this particular occasion, Randy's charm didn't help. The General recalled lightheartedly the time he was scheduled to be a guest of honor at an enlisted Marine's Dining Out (a formal military function that includes dinner).

Typically, these functions require a very formal uniform. As the story goes, when General Arick went for an afternoon run, Randy dutifully double checked the appropriate uniform requirements. It was a good thing as he was told, "…it is the White Mess Dress, not the evening Dress."

Randy quickly called the general who upon hearing this remarked, "That's great, my Mess Dress needs cleaning."

The general directed Randy to find out what other uniforms were being worn to which the unit commander replied, "The enlisted Marines will be wearing Dress Alphas but the general can wear anything he wants."

Upon hearing this, the general said, "Get my Alphas ready; I'll be there in fifteen minutes."

Randy ensured General Arick was ready and had his driver get him there on time. Keep in mind the general was actually in the wrong uniform. However, all good Marines, like their civilian counterparts, know that *a General Officer can theoretically never be in the wrong uniform. And, in this particular case, General Arick was a huge hit as the enlisted members thought he had dressed in that uniform to be a part of them!*

General Arick took this faux pas in stride, after all it wasn't the end of the world to be in the "wrong uniform" for dinner. Randy on the other hand, the true professional he is, went back to work to figure out how to ensure this would never happen again – not on his watch.

General Arick reflected, "Back then, like now with all of his challenges, Randy responded well and rebounded quickly."

Terry added, "We're amazed at how the family has persevered through this challenge. Kim, Nicole, and Kyle are all saints and Randy of course is a super hero." On a more personal note, she added how she and her husband had, "…enjoyed the most delightful lunch of grilled salmon prepared by Kim" when they last visited the Heberts and took a walk down Randy's Way.

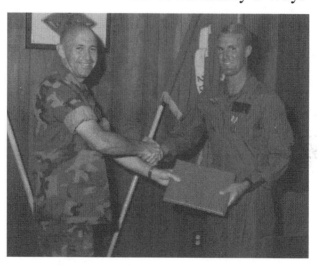

General John Arick recognizing Randy

part two

IT TAKES AN ISLAND

chapter eleven

RUNNING ON EMPTY

"A smooth sea never made a skillful sailor."

President Franklin D. Roosevelt

In 1977, a California baby boomer, singer, and song writer, perhaps better known for his 1983 soulful, "Tender is The Night," Jackson Browne released "Running on Empty." A folksy song about a single guy down on his luck reflecting on how his life and others' lives are empty, he has to decide what to do to survive. As the disease progressed it was unknown if Randy would live more than the average two to five years like most ALS patients. Certainly no one, except perhaps Randy and Kim, expected them to be sharing this story decades later. But in the mid-1990s, they too were emotionally and physically running on empty. Thankfully, friends from around the world unknowingly, perhaps inspired and led by the magnetism called Randy's Way, came together to lift up this family and share the load.

Living at the beach, island residents who own boats or just lay out on hot beaches, know only too well the importance of having an occasional nice breeze. Author Thomas S. Monson wrote, "We can't direct the wind, but we can adjust the sails." Perhaps he was talking about

the May 1993 "three-hour tour" when Randy and
Kim joined their good friends, Doctor Henry and
his wife, now retired, Marine Colonel Annita Best
on a similar voyage. Thankfully this tour didn't
end up like the 70's "Gilligan's Island" castaways
but it does begin to show how they all pitched in to
solve problems. The four were much younger then
and enjoying the seemingly *carefree* pre-ALS
diagnosis life of young adulthood. Henry had a
thriving medical practice while Annita, one of
Kim's best friends, and Randy, were young career-
minded Marine officers enjoying living at the
beach not too far away from the nearby military
installations. Just like the television show, this day
started out with a *Carolina Blue* sky and calm
water.

   "Let's go," Henry said about nine o'clock as
they talked about sailing his catamaran. Expecting
to be gone for less than three hours, no one thought
to pack food or drinks as they raced to the sixteen-
foot twin hull Hobie Cat waiting in the sand of
their beachfront home. No kids to worry about;
this was going to be relaxing and fun. As the four
of them coaxed the boat into the surf, they pushed
together until waist deep. Once it was floating on
top of the waves, they hopped aboard while Henry
skillfully angled the craft to catch the prevailing
wind. Setting the tandem rudders, they let God
provide the power to fill the sails as Henry guided
them seaward. The mainsail's rainbow colors

added to the excitement as they moved swiftly into deeper waters. The sea remained calm, with just enough breeze to navigate, allowing the boaters to enjoy the smooth ride as they sat on the webbed trampoline fixed between the hulls. Jellyfish bobbed effortlessly in the water made crystal clear with the cloudless sky. Nearly two miles offshore in a medium size boat without a motor might be concerning for some but this quartet was perfectly content. Then the breeze stopped.

Now they were drifting two miles offshore – nothing had changed – *or had it?*

Much like the song says, they were *Running on Empty* and without power those two miles might seem more like twenty.

In retrospect, Henry remembers thinking, *the wind will pick back up.*

Annita remembers thinking, *we have a babysitter and I don't want to have to pay more for being late.*

Floating around on the open ocean without food and drink with the sun high and lunch time approaching, well, one gets an increased sense of urgency.

As the sails hang listlessly, Annita asks, "Now what are we going to do?"

Henry responds, "I think we are going to have to paddle. Or wait for the wind to pick up."

So, the guys did what every other warm-blooded American male would do. *The women paddled in.* Seriously, they began to paddle the catamaran the entire two miles to the beach.

Wait a minute! Two young bikini clad women, each laid on their individual hull at the front of the boat and, using only their hands, reached over and paddled the boat back to shore? When did southern chivalry disappear?

Yep. Henry remembers starting with, "I can't paddle, I have to steer."

Randy quickly adds, "I can't either. My shoulder hurts." *Remember, this is coming from hard charging, fitness freak, combat veteran, Randy Hebert. Isn't it amazing how husbands, even Marines, can sometimes demonstrate frailty in front of wives and close friends; but not in front of others?*

Well, both ladies assumed their painful prostrate paddling positions. Inch by inch they progressed toward the shoreline praying the wind would pick up a little bit – it didn't. The one and a half hours it took to sail out using invisible energy provided by Venti, the Roman wind god, was surely going to take longer to get back under woman power.

Ever fearless women, Annita and Kim took stock at their present situation and decided this would serve as an additional session to their ever-present fitness regimen, while abled-body physician, Henry, "had to steer" and Randy "was injured." Settling into a rhythm, the girls started talking about the recent Clint Eastwood thriller, *Forgiven*. Henry and Annita had not seen it so Randy said he could tell them about it, if desired. Several hours later, after Randy talked nearly nonstop, the wind finally picked up and they finally glided ashore. By then, Henry and Annita knew every part of the movie. Twenty-five years later, they say Randy's regaling them as they propelled their way back to shore made it seem as if, "They had actually seen the movie," sans popcorn.

The bottom line is that even when the wind dies and your life turns upside down each of us can play an important part in solving life's challenges. Sometimes the part one plays won't be what's anticipated. Each of the four friends used their personal skills and talents to ensure they safely made it back to the island. In this case, even when his arm was hurting, although an unknown precursor to his ALS diagnosis, Randy helped the ladies forget about their own aching arms, throbbing leg muscles, and tightening backs, as they paddled safely back to shore.

chapter twelve

WALK TO "D'FEET" ALS

"Only God can turn a mess into a message, a test into a testimony, a trial into a triumph, a victim into a victory!"

Author Unknown

ALS attacks unknowing humans fourteen times a day, every day, around the globe. The killer sneaks up on its victims and slowly strangles their muscular control until they die. Sure, this is blunt. Some might say too terrifying a description of ALS, but one must face facts. Another startling data point, unless you currently live with or around someone suffering with Lou Gehrig's disease, is the fifteen human beings daily who die from the effects of this silent stalker. If you think it can't happen to you, ask around. Kim and Randy certainly had no idea, even though one of their relatives has since died from ALS. A future best friend of Kim's, Kelly Rogers, didn't even know what ALS was when unexpectedly, Brian, her new husband of only six months, received his devastating diagnosis.

It was a blessing when the Marine Corps relocated Randy and Kim back to Emerald Isle. Nearer to family and friends, they were also closer to the medical facilities that would become so important to Randy for the next twenty-five years. They sought answers as the mysterious illness ravaged his body causing him to lose control of his arms and eventually all his body. Their diagnosis, like Brian's, was just as bleak. Few people survive more than three years and they planned to make the best of them.

The irony of Kelly and Kim, both young; recently married; attending Chapel by the Sea at Emerald Isle, a small non-denominational church; with athletic husbands afflicted with ALS, is a bit uncanny. *Or, perhaps it is not at all.* I wonder if God didn't play a part in introducing these ladies. Kelly came to Emerald Isle from a small town near Durham, North Carolina and had married her high school sweetheart. Like Randy, Brian was a jock from a small Carolina town flaunting long white-blond hair, GQ preppy clothes, and fitness; Kelly is likewise, a beautiful southern belle. *Sound familiar?* Ironically, like Randy there is even a chemical connection as Brian was always around chemicals while working summers in golf course maintenance during high school and college. Unfortunately, during their honeymoon, Brian felt something was not right as he could not close the sliding door to their room. Within six months they knew he had ALS.

Because of the closeness of mutual friends on the island, the two ladies met in late 1996 and soon after, the couples were sharing time together.

Kim recalls, "Randy was about a year ahead of Brian at the time." Maybe they got along because of the adage, "Misery enjoys company."

Kelly remembers it differently. "Kim called me the day after the four of us first met and told me, "I'm your friend and will walk with you." At the time, neither realized how long the journey would be nor how many walks they would take together. Brian took a slightly different path than Randy. He chose to have a child, knowing he was ill and would likely die before she grew up, and he wanted to fully enjoy her as long as possible. Brian cherished their daughter and extended his life to be with Eason. Brian once pragmatically said, "There is a difference in being alive and living."

Like other chronic and terminal illness causes, people are always raising money and seeking awareness to find a cure. Little Emerald Isle, with fewer than 4,000 residents, is no different. It wanted to play a role in helping Randy, Brian's family, and others who have lost the fight to ALS. What is different in this tight knit community is the voracity this island took to battle for a cure. Perhaps it is because of its proximity to three Marine installations with daily flyovers of our beaches and because one of the main players in this drama is a retired Marine. Or perhaps it is the perfect storm of two women with strong convictions and desire to honor their husbands. Kim and Kelly played these roles well as they realized their common bond and ALS met the dynamic duo.

Over a nine-year period, the K-team relentlessly organized annual walks raising over one half a million dollars to aid in finding and funding awareness and a cure for ALS. Let's put that into perspective. With no fund-raising experience and situated at the end of North Carolina's Southern Outer Banks where the only living creatures to the east and south have fins, gills, and no money, these ladies raised more money that Raleigh or Charlotte, their big sister cities to the west. Raising money for continued research under the auspices of the Jim "Catfish" Hunter Chapter in Raleigh, key financial supporters such as Kim's dear friend Georgia Ricks and Kelly's mother in law, Ann White, helped the small group of islanders made a permanent and indelible mark on ALS fundraising. Years later, when a young man wanting to honor his deceased father, an ALS victim, with a cross-country fund-raising bike ride called Continental Crusade, asked where to start his ride, he was adamantly told, "Emerald Isle."

"The ALS Association picked our island for a good reason," according to Kim. Former Mayor, Art Schools, added, "There is a tremendous amount of community spirit in Emerald Isle…" Just like the five ALS events Kim and Kelly co-chaired, the Coast to Coast ride send-off was hosted at the world-famous Holiday Trav-L-Park. Ronnie Watson and his daughter, Tammy, along with their entire park staff, have made it their mission to support these types of causes ever since Ronnie served as the first Emerald Isle mayor. Humble in accepting praise, they donated their time, funds, and facility, located right on the beach, for the inspirational Emerald Isle ALS 5K run/walks, allowing thousands of participants, including hundreds of Marines from Randy's former unit, to assemble and begin their journeys.

"Life with ALS is not easy," Kim wrote, yet she and Kelly found the strength, time, and energy to support others by organizing walks and providing for continued research. Kim recounted how one morning she thought about what a blessing it is being able to wake up and put her feet on the floor. She admitted she was ashamed about taking that for granted, as many people might be. Finally, Kim shared how lying across from her in their bedroom with his eyes taped shut because they would dry out otherwise, she doesn't even know if her husband is asleep or not. He can't even move when he is awake, but he can and does always smile – every single day! This is where Kim finds the strength to carry on and fight for her husband, just as Kelly did. Spearheading this passion-filled endeavor together strengthened their relationships, while these Earth Angels served as compassionate and knowing listeners for each other. Kim added, "I do know without faith this road would be very rocky. My prayer is that every family suffering with ALS will also find salvation and a community filled with faithful, compassionate, loving friends…"

Randy, Kim & Melanie run to defeat ALS

Marines HUMPING on EI to support ALS research

chapter thirteen

A LITTLE HELP FROM MY FRIENDS

"How much love inside a friend? Depends on how much you give em."

Shel Silverstein

John Lennon and Paul McCartney of The Beatles fame have been inspirational to millions of people around the world. Poetically challenging the system, they gave youth of the 60s and 70s a voice to trumpet causes which certainly included fighting world injustices. Written specifically for Beatles drummer Ringo Starr, *A little help from my friends*, is precisely how Randy and Kim have persevered for nearly twenty-five years. Listen closely with your inner ear and you just might hear Ringo as he sings about the improbability of singing out of key. Stay in the moment and you might be fortunate enough to also hear co-composer Paul McCartney join Stevie Wonder at the keyboard in their 1982 classic, *Ebony and Ivory*, also implying that friendship, as in perfect harmony, is important in learning to survive.

The chapter title lyrics may also suggest why Randy fought the Department of Defense and the Department of Veterans Affairs. As a Marine field grade officer, he shared, with the entire world, why he felt so many of his fellow service members were succumbing to Gulf War Syndrome illnesses. Quite simply it was "MONEY."

Ironically, The Bible, in 1 Timothy 6:10 (KJV), and rocker, Pink Floyd, in his hit single, *Money*, agree that "The love of money is the root of all evil."

Randy used his voice and when he could no longer speak, like at the congressional hearings, the voices of Kim and his father, to help other veterans. Over the past twenty plus years others have been helping him. Like the Beatles' song or the hit television show, "Friends," Randy and the Hebert family have been constantly embraced by a wonderful, caring, diverse, and exceptionally supportive cast of friends. To capture all of them in this book is nearly impossible. Remember, almost everyone claims to be Randy's "best friend."

Rucker Johns (RJ) is a well-known family focused Emerald Isle restaurant with expansions in nearby Wilmington and Greenville. One summer afternoon, Randy and Kim's former neighbors, Polly Rucker Johns and Chris Johns, shared delightful stories about their good friends. Polly remembered how Kim was a young RJ waitress when handsome Marine officer Randy Hebert began, "Waiting for her at the bar." All of them, about the same age, started spending time together, including tanning on the "concrete beach" after Randy got sick.

Chris related how Randy, even though his speech was failing, shared the horror of the war and the anguish about what might be in store for his men. A "toxic cocktail" is what Randy called this exposure to chemicals during the war when describing his experiences. But there were and still are plenty of fun times.

With a wry smile, Polly described the "U-Haul Ramp" story. As their family grew, Chris and Polly relocated to nearby Pelletier. Randy, by now totally incapacitated, wanted to see the new home. Not a problem, except for the six steps they would have to maneuver to get Randy into the house. Nearly impossible with his heavy wheelchair!!! Nearly.... His friends nervously agreed to Randy's suggestion that they place him in the back of the U-Haul and drive to the house. Once there, you guessed it, they pulled out the ramp and, "with a little help from my friends," Randy rode right into the house. Humorously, while Randy waited in the U-Haul, the Johns' beagle puppy jumped into the back of the truck and was nearly licking him to death until Kim and Chris' rescue.

If you have ever experienced a life threatening or altering surgery, you probably remember the day before as your senses were on high alert trying to remember every sight, smell, or touch. Randy's "last supper" just before he had his tracheotomy was with friends at their home. They did it right for Randy, steaming nearly ten pounds of crab legs and cracking every piece Randy could consume. While Randy has not been able to eat solid food for twenty years, they still go out with friends to Rucker Johns and other area restaurants to socialize and enjoy great company.

Friends have been equally important to Kim and nothing says "friends" like the group of women Kim hangs around with. Probably all wives, if honest with themselves, would say they need a break from time to time. Thick as thieves, her girlfriends even convince Kim to join them for occasional shopping sprees or perhaps out of town, overnight adventures. They once had a girls' night out to celebrate Kim's fortieth birthday; *let's just say that was a couple of years ago*. It might have been easy for the ladies on the island to have forgotten others with this illness, but Randy and Kim are so imbedded in the community their friends desire them in their lives.

Friends…, like Dorla and Charlie Pake who once lived right down the street from the Heberts. Stories filled the room as each recounted their past quarter century with the Hebert family. In addition to helping fill in the gaps where Randy's physicality would not allow, such as hunting or surfing with Kyle, Charlie and Dorla provided support to both spouses. One funny memory was when the couples were going out to eat dinner. Charlie and the others went to the van and found that the wheelchair ramp would not cooperate. Try as they might, none of them could figure it out. Then Charlie saw what he refers to as, Randy "Blinking Out."

Think about it. You can't talk and are sitting motionless while you know the answer. But, no one is paying any attention to you for one of a million reasons.

In this case, Charlie finally noticed Randy was blinking to get their attention and tell them how to fix the ramp.

The Juggler, Bill Flynn is another fine example of a good friend. After spending time with this retired FBI special agent, one might want to belly up to the bar with this "Cheers"- like character and share some stories. Mysterious and interesting are words that could describe how Randy and this special agent, who had been assigned in big cities like Chicago, Detroit and Manhattan, began their relationship. *I believe it was Divine Intervention.* They met back in 1999 when Bill was working at Camp Lejeune and decided to live in Emerald Isle. A good friend asked Bill if he might like to fill in as a reading backup with Randy. Soon after, Bill became the principal reader which is critical as Randy continues to have a thirst for learning and enjoys good books. Imagine all the stories one could tell if you have been reading with someone for two decades.

Initially they would read formally one hour a week while now like good friends some of their "readings" turn into "BS" sessions. In the first year, Bill thought he was boring Randy and putting him to sleep. Like me, Bill didn't really understand all the ALS nuances and didn't realize Randy's eyes were bothering him making it appear he was trying to sleep. On one occasion however, one of them really did fall asleep. And, it wasn't Randy. Bill had been putting in long hours in other ventures while still finding time to read with Randy. Sure enough, he was so exhausted, Bill fell asleep while reading aloud and woke up only when he dropped the book.

Like others, Bill said, "I get much more than I give," during visits with Randy. "A book entitled *Juggling for the Klutz* sat on my desk for nearly thirty years. Finally, one day I decided to learn how to juggle so I could show Randy." Picture this sixty-something retired FBI agent learning to juggle just to show his wheelchair bound friend – that is the definition of friendship!

With tears in his eyes, David Dorworth, another Emerald Isle neighbor, remembered when Randy told him, "At least with this affliction I'll be able to watch my children grow up." His wife, Vicki, and adult son, Tyler, are special friends who have enjoyed their beach house, just up the road from Randy and Kim, for decades. Randy taught Tyler, now in his mid-twenties, how to ride a bike even though Randy was already suffering the early effects of his illness. Once again, I heard that Randy was their "Best friend." Tyler remembered when he was about three years old how this uncle-like figure picked him up when he fell off his bike while learning to ride. Vicki vividly remembered Randy jogging down, unannounced and uninvited, to help her carry a new mattress up two flights of stairs into their beach home. *Like many wives say of their husbands, David was on a trip when the heavy lifting needed to be accomplished.*

Genuine, serious and focused, Vicki and David care for Randy and Kim much like parent figures. *Okay, maybe big brother and sister.* Just like family, they hurt then and now. David said, "Randy and Kim have been sadly robbed of their youth and lives through our generation's Agent Orange" which sickened our Vietnam era troops with long-lasting effects like the toxic chemicals did in the Gulf War.

Vicki said, "Kim never gives up – she has a sixth sense of fighting bureaucracy...", while Tyler added, "Randy is an inspiration to me. It is so impressive how he has been there for his kids."

116

David said, "In the last conversation we shared before Randy was unable to speak he said to me, 'I believe ALS will be cured but possibly not in my lifetime.'"

Many friends have remained steadfast and constant in Randy's life such as Jill Wilson, one of his earliest island friends, having met in 1986. Jill ran a beach umbrella business and well, Randy was always on the beach if not working. Through the years, Jill remains close with Randy and Kim, including providing massages to Randy, writing a case study about his experience while she was in college, and learning to use the ABC method in the winter of 2005. Like Jill, there have been so many others through the decades including their entire Chapel by the Sea congregation of friends.

Being a transplanted North Carolinian, like the Carole King soft rock ballad popularized by James Taylor in 1971, "...Ain't it good to know you've got a friend..."

chapter fourteen

FIFTY-SEVEN CENTS

"Nothing is impossible; the word itself says

I'M POSSIBLE."

Audrey Hepburn

While Randy and Kim receive incalculable help from their friends across the world and especially on the island, they give back in spades. Highlighting one quick example of this payback includes another Marine general, who happened to live across the street. It is vitally important for readers, unfamiliar with the military, to appreciate that becoming a general, especially in the much smaller military branch of the Marine Corps, is a feat unto itself. Generals may be revered and, in some minds, even put on a pedestal above reproach. Like a Sergeant Major, they know everything, or maybe not.

Retired Marine Major General Gregg Sturdevant and his wife, Tina, moved across the street several years after Randy was in full blown ALS. They really didn't know Randy as a young, hard-charging Marine officer. But General Sturdevant knew his reputation. Eventually, they became good friends sharing dinner at local island restaurants. General Sturdevant quickly found out

118

Randy was as smart as a whip and known to be able to fix anything.

One day, after working tirelessly to solve a personal dilemma he resorted to asking Randy. As he and Tina often did, General Sturdevant walked across the street to check in with Randy who was sitting on the driveway enjoying the afternoon sunshine. Communicating through the ABC method, the general admitted to Randy he was having trouble fixing his broken toilet. The conversation went sort of like this,

"Randy, I need your help."

"Okay General, what's the problem?"

"I've been trying to keep my toilet from running for the past few hours. I've replaced all the guts but it just won't stop."

"Understood Sir. Have you checked to ensure the washer under the flapper is seated?"

"Nope. Didn't realize it was there."

"Okay. General, go to ACE Hardware on the island, pick one up and replace it. Let me know how it works when you finish."

Remember, this entire conversation takes place through a nurse using a personally designed process and likely took five or more minutes.

Time went by and the general left for a business trip. A month or so later he was back home and walked over to visit with Randy.

After checking in Randy asked, "General, how's the toilet?"

General Sturdevant replied, "Randy, you were right. I owe you! Thanks so much."

"Glad to help Sir. What did it cost you?"

Gulping, the general replied, "Fifty-seven cents."

Who would have thought a man with ALS for over twenty years would be able to help repair a Marine Corps General's toilet while sitting immobile in a wheelchair across the street?

chapter fifteen

FIRE IN THE CHIMNEY

"Truly, God works in mysterious ways. The wheels of His mercy and justice move quietly, but they do move."

Billy Graham

Just when you thought you've seen everything, your house burns down. Haven't you heard about people or families who keep getting hit squarely on the chin so many times you wonder if they have the proverbial black cloud hanging over them? Then again, if you have faith in God, you know he only gives you what you can handle. If your faith is weak or perhaps you are not sure, it may feel as if He is filling your backpack with one hundred pounds of rocks and asking you to go on a hundred-mile march. As a human, one might feel overburdened, but as a child of God, one should feel as if they are completing their challenges on earth as they prepare for the afterlife.

Picture this real-world challenge the Hebert family faced in the fall of 2003. Kim's beloved father, the patriarch of their family who was otherwise extremely healthy, unexpectedly died. Nearly eight years into their ALS struggle, the small family is sent reeling once again as Dad and Grandpa is suddenly taken from them shattering dreams and upending the "new normal" they had adjusted to.

Kim's mom began to spend more time on the island, staying overnight occasionally at Randy's house just a few miles away from her home. She couldn't bear to be there without her soulmate. As we reflect on how she came to be at Randy's home this evening one can easily believe this was God's plan. The story continues with a nice warming fire in the fireplace providing comfort and fighting the chill of a cold January night. As the evening waned, so did the fire. Surprisingly, for a weeknight, both Randy and Kim were awake keeping Mom company.

Over the next few hours, as the fire smoldered, Kim's mom kept hearing a strange noise thinking perhaps it might be a bird or even a squirrel clambering in the chimney. Kim was struggling to stay awake and ignored her mom's concerns. As Kim tried to doze before heading upstairs to help Randy into bed her mom kept waking her up. Certainly no one suspected what was about to happen. Finally, her mom's alarms captured Kim's full attention.

Wearing her winter pajamas, Kim quickly peeked out the front door. Seeing quite a bit of smoke above their house, she raced further out on the deck and looked up. The chimney was ablaze as flames licked the rooftop. Grabbing her phone,

Kim called her dear friend and neighbor, Charlie Pake, saying, "I think our house is on fire."

As his house sat on a hill down the road, he was able to glance out his window and see Kim's roof. Charlie confirmed their fears yelling, "Holy Shit, it is! Kim, get out." Charlie raced up the road to the house and helped them evacuate, arriving just ahead of the fire department which quickly sped down the island. All knew Randy and Kim and the challenges they faced in a house fire.

After alerting the fire department, Kim had yelled for the kids to wake up and get outside. Grandma ran upstairs and ushered the kids leaving Kim to work feverishly to get Randy to the elevator and down to the ground floor. Thankfully Kim and Randy had stayed up longer than usual keeping Mom company or they might have been overcome by smoke.

Fighting icy and freezing conditions, Captain Bruce Norman and twelve firefighters from three neighboring departments quickly developed their plan of action. Kim urged them to save her home and especially one priceless possession, a unique chalk portrait of Randy and the kids which an artist had completed merging two separate photographs. This memento is the only example of a healthy Randy in his Marine uniform with the kids sitting on his lap. Because of Charlie's quick action and the response of the Emerald Isle fire department, the Hebert home and belongings were saved although it took nearly half a year to complete the necessary house repairs.

God was absolutely involved in saving the Hebert family and their belongings. As we have heard repeatedly about more recent disasters, "You can replace your home but you can't replace your lives." God was also involved in the second act of this drama called Fire in the Chimney. As the family moved out to a small house in nearby Spinnaker's Reach, their friends rallied, even building a ramp for Randy to easily access the temporary home.

As if they had not had enough cloudy weather, the insurance company was balking at paying their repair claim. *Time for another miracle; this time from former Presidential candidate Ross Perot, Senior.* Mr. Perot happened to be well connected with the Hebert's insurance company and somehow happened to become aware that they were having difficulty getting the claim resolved. Once apprised, Mr. Perot placed an immediate call to Kim that went something like,

"Kim. Ross Perot here."

"Excuse me," she replied.

"Yes, Ross Perot. I understand you are having trouble with your insurance company. I don't care about the details. Just tell me what you need and let's get it done!"

Gulping and realizing that another Texan, like Randy, and a very sincere billionaire who has financed health related research on Gulf War veterans, was on the other end of this conversation, Kim responded, "Yes sir Mr. Perot, this is Kim Hebert. And yes, we have not had good luck with getting the insurance company to cover our house repair claim."

"I'll call you back in ten minutes Kim."

Sure enough, he did. All the insurance claim issues were magically resolved. Actually, we prefer this not really be considered *magic*. We believe this was another example of God's Grace.

Even this was not the end of the fire story as a few months later the same Mr. Perot, a Naval Academy graduate and American patriot, reentered the Hebert's lives. In March 2004, Mr. Perot introduced Randy and Kim when they were honored at the national "Voices Take Flight" ALS Awareness event in Arizona.

And remember Charlie, the neighbor who ensured everyone got out safely by racing to the rescue? Charlie recounted a beautiful story he later told Randy about how he had died when he was barely fourteen years old. Charlie loves to ski on the water and slopes. Once, while young and living in Canada, he was skiing on closed slopes with some teenaged friends. This slope was called suicide hill for obvious reasons. Before his final run, as Charlie pulled on his parka, he heard in the distance a deep threatening rumble growing quickly into a deafening roar. Suddenly, more quickly than imaginable, an avalanche of snow engulfed Charlie. As the girls in the group raced to get help, the boys started digging. During the time he was trapped and unconscious, Charlie remembers his life flashing before him.

"I saw the tunnel we've all heard about. As I walked down the tunnel and reached for His hand, I was pulled back and out of the snow bank."

Charlie was back, breathing and alive. But, he knew then, and now, that to die is not the end, but the beginning. Years later, as he raced to help Kim and Randy evacuate, Charlie knew he would eventually need to share his story with Randy.

chapter sixteen

THE CONTRACTOR

"You can learn so much just by observing."

Jessica Williams

Everybody should have a Cousin Mike! By our definition this person is always available to help and is usually skilled with home repairs, typically related by blood or marriage, gregarious, selfless with resources and time, offers ideas and suggestions to help (whether you use them or not), doesn't wear his emotions on his sleeve, and is generally just a good ole boy. Our Cousin Mike (Logan) is all of those although the last description may be argued since he originally hails from north of the Mason-Dixon line.

Many, many people have helped build and rebuild the family beach home after the fire and later when they needed to improve handicap accessibility. But Cousin Mike has been a mainstay and always available, at the drop of a hat, to run over and see, "why the garage door won't open," "what's wrong with the circuit breaker," or any number of other issues. He is the consummate fix-it man which is why he stays so busy with his own contracting business. Whenever Randy and Kim need their home renovated Cousin Mike gets the call.

Keep in mind that Randy is a trained Combat Engineer with a great mind for project management and his dad is also a gifted designer. Couple that with a strong-willed expert and you have the ingredients for a perfect storm. In every expansion or remodeling project Randy has been directly involved including determining which materials to use, the cost of the project, and approving the outcome. Sitting totally still in a wheelchair does not define Randy. It just makes it more cumbersome to navigate construction sites. In one project Randy spent months, along with his dad, designing and drafting drawings for their right-side house expansion – no small undertaking for even an able-bodied man. Randy "ABCed," which one might consider the ultimate whisper game, to communicate his desires through nurses.

Getting detailed building plans accurately communicated through a nurse or aid who does not understand drawings or project management was a huge accomplishment. But, they did it and Cousin Mike came to complete the project. He had worked with Randy previously and knew what it was like to be under constant scrutiny and observation. This was a gargantuan remodel and he wasn't really looking forward to having an unpaid, owner, overseer on this job. Well, Randy also wasn't planning on *not* being involved. Like in the 1970 spacecraft incident made famous by the 1995 movie, Apollo 13, we sort of, "…have a problem."

As Cousin Mike got started with the remodeling, Randy asked a nurse to hand Mike four or five pages of probably one hundred or more basic steps which Randy expected to be followed. Mike quickly glanced at the list, went to his van and tossed them in, without a care. A week or so later, another nurse was trying to tell Cousin Mike something, but it was obvious she didn't understand what she was saying. Finally, Cousin Mike got it. Randy was saying to check something on page 3, line 187. From his wheelchair, without even looking at the list, Randy was communicating a concern he wanted checked out. Another time, Randy was telling Cousin Mike that a newly installed window was off-center. Keep in mind that Randy could sit for hours upon hours watching every event unfold and knew what he wanted. In this case, Cousin Mike was not pleased to be questioned on a construction task such as a window being installed incorrectly. He re-measured it and restated, "It isn't off." But in the end, it was Randy's unique perspective and reflective nature that won out as he was correct when observing the window -- from the outside.

Their relationship wasn't all work. If one individual enjoys humor in the face of challenges it is Cousin Mike who has endured his own personal tragedies. Once, even after Randy got sick, Cousin

Mike took him to the Star Hill Golf Course in nearby Cape Carteret. Kim told them to drive the conversion van as it would be easier to get Randy in and out -- for someone that is comfortable with the van. Cousin Mike was not. Those of us who golf also realize most golf carts don't come with seat belts.

Mike remembered, "My challenge was how do I get Randy out of the van, into the golf cart without letting him fall, and then move the van. Then, how do I drive around the course with all the hills and keep Randy in the cart. I figured it out eventually. As it turns out, while I was driving the golf cart, I put my right arm around Randy to hold him in as we drove to each hole. The entire day people were yelling, 'Hi, Randy' as he was quite popular."

That was interesting enough but what happened next was more so. On one of the holes Mike parked close to the green so he could jump out, putt, and get back to the cart. He's not sure exactly what happened but apparently Randy moved his left leg, placing the cart in gear. Mike caught a glimpse of Randy as he took off headed straight for a white picket fence. Randy crashed right into it, thankfully was not hurt, and never told Cousin Mike whether he meant to put it in gear. Randy was knowingly laughing however when Mike finally caught him.

Cousin Mike, Eugene Sanford (Randy's father-in-law), friend & Randy

***

"What is the shortest word in the English language that contains the letters: abcdef? FEEDBACK. Don't forget that feedback is one of the essential elements of good communication."

Author anonymous

chapter seventeen

THANKSGIVING & FOOTBALL: HEBERT STYLE

"You don't choose your family. They are God's gift to you, as you are to them."

Desmond Tutu

Originating in football-rich Texas, many of the Hebert clan are die-hard Dallas Cowboy fans. Randy has long admired Roger Staubach, perhaps the best-known Cowboy. It doesn't hurt that Staubach was the 1963 Heisman Trophy winner while graduating from the United States Naval Academy, won two Super Bowl championships, was the National Football League Man of the Year in 1978, and served his country as a Naval officer during a combat tour in Vietnam. Randy and Roger had many things in common: fitness, football, military, and Texas to name a few. One of Randy's prized possessions is a picture in his man cave of Roger Staubach which was won at an auction and presented to Randy by his favorite ALS physician, Dr. Richard Bedlack.

The family moved circuitously to South Carolina and well I guess one might say you can take the Heberts out of Texas but you can't take Texas and football out of the Heberts.

Thanksgiving dinners and annual football games are no exception. Just like the feel-good, made for television movies that air around the holidays, the Hebert annual Thanksgiving reunion contains all the drama, love, and delicious food.

Long before Randy became ill, Melanie's husband, Bill, also a stellar athlete and equally competitive, urged the family to play a holiday football game. In 1987, when Randy returned from his military tour in Okinawa, the first game was played near Greenville, South Carolina at Eastside High School where Randy played safety on the high school football team. Bill recalls they planned to play two-hand touch as everybody, including Randy's parents, siblings, neighbors, and friends participated. Bill fondly remembered how, "People started getting back in shape early, primarily because Randy would be judgmental and just like in elementary school no one wanted to be picked last for either team."

Typical of Randy and Bill, there were formal rules including time outs, a two second counting rule for rushing the quarterback, and colored shirts to identify the teams. Until 1991 the spirited games became more and more competitive with Randy bringing a Navy SEAL friend to play and Bill enlisting the help of a friend who just happened to be a high school quarterback. These were serious games. Even Randy's mom, Shirdale, or Dolly as she sometimes is referred to, sported a black eye from the inaugural game and couldn't wait to get back to work to show her office mates. Another example of family competitive spirit is when team Captain Bill Crawford pulled his hamstring fumbling the ball as he collapsed to the ground. His dear wife, Melanie, happened to be in a position to recover the ball and did so. Did she stop to check on her injured husband? Nope! With the maiden name of Hebert and her familial genes flowing through her, Melanie laughingly ran the ball back for a touchdown before checking on Bill. He was on the opposing team after all.

The scheduled two-hour games always started and stopped on time, but during the game, time didn't always matter to Randy. Bill recalls yelling at Randy, who used index cards for designing and sharing plays with his team, "Come on. My clothes are going out of style," or "What's taking so long; I'm going to sleep over here." Randy told me that his strategy and planning worked as he won most of the games. Since this is Randy's story we'll leave that debate to those who played.

Fast forward to 1994 and Randy had returned from the war. During the game, Randy struggled to pass the ball and told people his, "Thumb was messed up."

Afterwards, Bill asked his brother-in-law, "What's going on?" to which Randy replied, "…hurt my back in a surfing accident." Bill responded, "Get that shit checked out." Neither really knew what was about to transpire.

Serious football games continued even as Randy began to worry about his fitness. Not being able to max out the Marine annual fitness test worried him -- he could now only do seventeen of the required twenty chin-ups to be considered perfect, which he had always accomplished previously. Soon after, he could only complete three. His downward fitness spiral had begun and was moving quickly. Even as he was being seen by Naval doctors and eventually diagnosed with ALS, Randy knew, "The game must go on." To ensure Randy could compete, the Thanksgiving celebration and more importantly the football game was moved to Emerald Isle the following year.

New friends, including Annita and Henry Best and many of Kyle and Nicole's classmates joined the family in continuing the tradition. When Randy could no longer hold the ball in his passing hand, he and his father designed a wired glove that allowed Randy to hold the ball and continue to play. Eventually, Randy became wheelchair bound yet still wanted to participate. So, he did the next best thing: he coached from the sideline.

"A healthy Randy was wide damn open; ninety miles per hour. Now, he had to sit on the sideline calling plays. It just didn't feel right," Bill recalled. "Randy was like a body trapped under a ton of bricks." While the annual game has since been called off, large groups of family and friends still gather for holiday celebrations.

Early Thanksgiving Football Game

Last Game Day with Melanie and Michelle

chapter eighteen

THOU SHALL NOT *CORVETTE*

"We make a living by what we get, but we make a life by what we give."

Winston Churchill

Randy's "cherry" corvette

Many of us learn in Sunday school that the tenth Commandment reads, "Thou shall not Covet." The Merriam Webster dictionary makes this clearer by defining covet as "to desire" (what belongs to another inordinately or culpably).

A corvette is exactly the type of possession one might covet. Let's allow a slight interpretation, asking in advance for God's forgiveness for our frailty in desiring somewhat unattainable objects of desire. Like the little drummer boy who gave everything he had to the Christ Child, perhaps the most selfless gift a person can give, short of their life for another human being, might very well be his most prized possession. In America, this is often a car. Particularly with Marines and other like groups of men, a vehicle is an extension or expression of oneself.

Pages ago we learned from Keith Meacham that Randy loved to drive fast. Many of Randy's friends talked about his fascination with speed and some even mentioned witnessing a few tickets. They all know of his obsession with cars including his BMW, Volkswagen, and his prized possession, a 1973 white Stingray convertible corvette with a beautiful camel interior. Randy was fortunate enough to purchase this cherry-condition road beast as a 1992 wedding present to himself from good friend Lieutenant Dave Dawson.

It isn't really coveting if you own it – is it? Randy owned this car and let everyone know it when he fired up the engine in his beachfront neighborhood early in the mornings so he could race the twenty-five miles down Freedom Highway to Camp Lejeune. He loved this car so much that when he got physically unable to open the inlaid door handles Randy secretly never closed them all the way. This "adapting and overcoming" attitude allowed Randy to get back in the car without anyone knowing he couldn't operate the door handle.

Unfortunately, Randy eventually was unable to control his arms and legs, and well, he just couldn't safely afford to be on the road in this machine – it would have been dangerous.

With the car sitting idle in the garage and his thirst for going to the beach continuing, Randy decided to make one of the hardest material decisions a man might ever make. Until now, Randy would get to the beach under his own power; sometimes assisted by able-bodied friends. They would help Randy up and down the steps which at the time were at every Emerald Isle beach access.

Hmmm. How can we kill two birds with one stone?

Randy and dear friend John Johnson "Big John" came up with a wonderfully selfless idea that made the island more accessible for all physically challenged visitors and residents. They thought that raffling off Randy's beloved corvette and using the money to build a wooden ramp with just the right slope and NO STEPS would be a perfect use for the car, especially since Randy couldn't drive anymore.

The weather on the day of the raffle was picture perfect. Emotions of course were mixed. Seven hundred and fifty tickets sold out within two weeks and the family and friends attending the raffle were in a celebratory mood. The event was awesome – remember, the car was in immaculate condition and the raffle was for a great cause! However, the cost for supplying the wood and materials for the three hundred and forty-foot long by six-foot wide ramp to the sand was more than anticipated. *By now you might guess what happened.* Randy and Kim's dear friends, Eddie and Donna McNeil, stepped in and covered the rest of the expenses. Eddie tried in vain to get Randy to keep the car and said he would cover all the costs.

When finished, *Randy's Way* was the island's first truly handicap accessible ramp.

Randy's Way in 2017

EI's initial handicap access beach path

Randy with corvette's proud new owner.

***

**"The great use of life is to spend it for
something that outlasts it."**

William James

Thomas P. Gill

part three

FINDING FAITH

chapter nineteen

"GOD DOESN'T MAKE MISTAKES"

"Even though I walk through the darkest valley, I will fear no evil, for you are with me; your rod and your staff, they comfort me."

Psalm 23:4 (NIV)

During my first interview with Randy, I asked, "Why are you still alive?" Some might think this was a bit blunt and maybe too direct, but one had to be there. And I needed to test the parameters if we were going to write an honest reflection that might be beneficial to others. Without hesitation, the nurse began spelling out Randy's response using their alphabet code which I had not quite figured out yet.

His equally direct reply was, "God doesn't make mistakes!" I knew immediately we would tell this story.

Throughout numerous ensuing interviews, the topic routinely turned to religion, although it may have run a close second to tanning. Both are widely important to Randy. In the earliest part of their marriage, Kim and Randy were practicing Catholics. While living in Missouri and knowing that something was physically wrong, but without a medical diagnosis, for one reason or another, they decided to try out a Baptist church located right outside the Fort Leonard Wood main gate.

Kim said, "The people were so welcoming and they invited us to a week-long revival. We went every single night and near the end a light bulb went off about salvation. We had missed the picture in other denominations." She remembered the revivalist saying, "All you have to do is ask for forgiveness and God will be there for you."

Later, when Kim asked Randy if he thought they would survive, he gave her peace in saying, "We have constant blessings." and "God will provide."

This relationship with God has been at the forefront of their marriage, their parenting, and being stewards of their resources and friendships. Emerald Isle's Chapel by the Sea senior pastor, Clay Olson, aptly describes Randy's "walk" with God as reflective of Mark 10:45 which says, "For even the Son of Man did not come to be served, but to serve and to give His life as a ransom for many." Finding fulfillment through the spirit, as well as in serving his fellow man continues today. A long-time member, Randy serves as an inspiration and demonstration of perseverance, "in the face of extreme hardship" to the entire congregation. *How many readers would look in the mirror and honestly say they would come to church if it took three hours just to get ready?*

Before Randy was incapacitated, he served as a cheerful example for coming to church. He often ran the five miles to the Men's Fellowship Group. Camaraderie with God-fearing men was equally, if not more, important to Randy as the camaraderie of war-fighting Marines. A dedicated role model before and now, Randy continues to love learning about the Lord of Lords and King of Kings. Some readers might forget that Randy was also a combat veteran—an officer dedicated to being the best of the best in terms of protecting his Marines and the United States. But his love for God is second to none. Even so, his toughness and fortitude are without question.

Pastor Clay added, "One of the things I remember at Randy's retirement party was hearing an officer describing the toughness of several other officers. Then there was Randy…"

Randy also believes, much like the famous southern statesman, General Robert E. Lee, "Kindness to children is of the highest importance." Even though a seasoned war veteran, Randy often substituted as a Sunday School teacher. Perhaps the kids saw that he was walking the walk and talking the talk -- the bottom line is they loved when Randy came to teach.

Reflecting on Randy as a parishioner, Pastor Clay recounted how Randy is aware that, "God knows our heart," and while he is limited now physically, his desire to do good for his family, church, and of course God, is known and credited. "He is the encourager of people who pray for him, share with him, and think of him."

Much like the mighty warrior, King David, who desired to build a temple, God knows Randy's heart. As Pastor Clay continued, "Even after all these years of being imprisoned in a body of affliction, he portrays a spirit of cheerfulness, courage, and encouragement to others." A role model for all people challenged or suffering, Randy believes Romans 8:38-39, "For I am convinced that neither death nor life, neither angels nor demons, neither the present nor the future, nor any powers, neither height nor depth, nor anything else in all creation, will be able to separate us from the love of God that is in Christ Jesus our Lord."

Randy's deep faith allows him to gracefully live in the face of death without fear. When asked, he responded, "I am not afraid to die, I just don't want to right now."

chapter twenty

MY MASTERPIECE

"For we are God's masterpiece. He has created us anew in Christ Jesus, so we can do the good things he planned for us long ago."

Ephesians 2:10 (NLT)

Brother-in-law Frank Snyder married into the Hebert family just a few years ago and frankly was a bit uncomfortable in visiting Randy and Kim. *As Melanie's husband, that wasn't going to last long.*

At one of their first dinners, sitting across from Kim, Randy "asked" if Frank was okay with the poodles lying at his feet.

Wow! Frank thought. Randy is more concerned about my well-being than his own. Being a deeply spiritual person, Frank had been stunned and has often thought about that brief encounter. He also thought of then professional football player Steve Gleason who played safety for the New Orleans Saints. Gleason is also battling ALS and like the Heberts, he and his wife Michel, were trying to conceive when he was diagnosed. While Randy is a die-hard Dallas Cowboys fan, the fact that Gleason was playing in bordering state Louisiana, where they know how to pronounce his name correctly, is something he might have overlooked. And like Randy's mission is to share his ALS journey as an encouraging and inspirational reflection, Gleason made a documentary film covering five years of his life as he battles the progressive stages of ALS.

As a furniture sales executive, Frank is on the road a lot and regularly stays in hotels. One time he was physically feeling bad and decided to pray about his scoliosis which he has suffered with for decades. As he prayed, God brought Randy to his mind.

God said to Frank, "Randy has taken what he was blessed and cursed with and has glorified Me!" God continued, "Ask Me how you can glorify Me! He (Randy) is my masterpiece."

Frank realized instantly he needs to be happy and pleased with what God has blessed him and not upset with those things that might be earthly challenges. *They actually may be blessings.* Frank shared, "I realize now that Randy has touched so many lives through his curse/blessing. He has since inspired me. His strength and courage are tremendous and I believe God is using Randy as an example of His glory and to give people Hope, the gift of Jesus Christ."

chapter twenty-one

VETERANS DAY BLESSING

"God gave you a gift of 86,400 seconds today. Have you used one to say Thank You?"

William Arthur Ward

One unique memory occurred on a special Veterans Day demonstrating that regardless of tragedies like the recent Las Vegas and Texas shootings the world is full of compassionate and caring people.

Picture this. After having just attended the Morehead City, North Carolina Veterans Day Parade, a small tribe of young kids, Kim, and of course Randy, ambled into the local Hardees restaurant. Kim recalls it was sort of like herding cats. Once she got the kids and Randy situated at the table, Kim ordered drinks and lots of little burgers.

As they finished their meal, without warning, a man quickly walked by and abruptly tossed a folded piece of paper on the table. He then raced out the door.

Kim thought she noticed that the man was crying as he sped to his nearby parked car. After quickly checking out the piece of paper, Kim sprinted out the door, catching the stranger in the parking lot before he could pull away.

The hand-written note simply said, "A Gift from God" and included a $2,000.00 check which he would not allow Kim to return. This saint had noticed the family in the restaurant as they were beginning to eat and humbly said, "This is my blessing to the family and veteran."

Miracles really do happen every day. Sometimes you just need to open your eyes.

chapter twenty-two

HEALING MIRACLES

"Miracles happen every day. Change your perception of what a miracle is and you'll see them all around you."

Jon Bon Jovi

As time moved on and Randy's condition deteriorated Kim was sometimes near frantic with worry. A dedicated mom, loyal wife, and most importantly devout Christian, she occasionally wondered *Why can't Randy have a healing miracle?* $2,000.00 checks and other wonderful miracles of assistance are nice, but what she/they really prayed for was a cure.

In 1996, they received their opportunity. Noted evangelist and spiritual healer, Benny Hinn's road trip would take him less than three hours away, to nearby Raleigh, North Carolina.

Kim remembered, "A few of our friends loaded into Randy's van and made the trip. With Randy in his wheelchair, we managed to get seats in the middle of Reynolds Coliseum. The climate was electric. Thousands of believers filled the seats praying for their own healing or for friends or family members they had accompanied. Pentecostals, with loud, unfamiliar chanting were seated beside more sedate and formally dressed believers. Protestants, Catholics, people of the Jewish faith, and many others were present; it was beautiful to know we were all praying to the same God, hoping for a miracle."

On stage, dressed in his traditional, near blinding, white outfit, Benny Hinn was captivating. The choir's music filled the room as thousands of people moved rhythmically to the beat. Mr. Hinn repeatedly and loudly said, "I do not heal you." He exclaimed, "Only the Lord will heal you; if it is his will!"

Like many others, Kim was enthralled, if not entranced. Kim just knew her prayers would be answered tonight. She had done everything she could possibly do, kept sacred her wedding vows, and was working hard to raise their children as Christians.

She shared, "People all around us prayed to be healed. I prayed the hardest I could that day and was only hoping Randy was praying as hard as I was. Until this day, I have wondered what others were praying for that they got healed and Randy was not chosen for the healing." *Perhaps God has more work for Randy to do?*

"I'm not sure what the answer is and why the Lord chooses some people to be healed. I guess when I get to heaven that might be the first question I want to ask." Kim ended saying, "It was an amazing day, very emotional, we laughed, we cried and we thanked God for the people that did get healed that day."

Ever wonder if maybe, just maybe, Randy and Kim got their miracle some twenty years ago...?

chapter twenty-three

"WELCOME TO THE CORPS"

"We love because he first loved us."

1 John 4:19 (NIV)

Randy (last Marine on left) "welcomes" Lisa to the Corps

Customary in a Marine Corps' wedding, one of the Marines in the wedding party will smack the new bride on the posterior with his sword and say, "Welcome to the Corps, Ma'am." Randy welcomed Lisa, Mike Braham's bride, into the Corps and Mike returned the honor and welcomed Kim when she married Randy. This honor often is afforded to someone who has the utmost respect of the groom and hopefully the new bride. In this case, both are true.

Like many of us, Mike had a different side to him as a young Marine officer. Now a "born-again" Christian, husband, and father, Mike was not as disciplined twenty-five years ago. Mike is also the individual who Randy sent a *Take Care of Kim* letter in case he did not return from the war and is the man Randy called when he needed to talk about losing strength in his arms after returning from the war. The bottom line, Mike knows Randy as well as anyone and shared valuable insights.

For example, while devout Christians, when Mike and Lisa visit Randy and Kim they often leave feeling they have been ministered to more than they shared. On one visit, Mike asked, "Have you accepted Christ as your Savior?" Randy smiled and responded, "I know the Lord."

Mike and Lisa visit Randy and Kim

Getting back to his, "Welcome to the Corps," Mike knows God placed this hard charging, focused, and sometimes difficult-to-please woman in Randy's life. He knew what was to happen and what was needed.

Mike said, "Kim has singularly kept Randy alive. I've seen her manhandle Randy in and out of the van – she's frickin' amazing!" In this regard, Mike and Kim pushed together to ensure Randy, his family, and other service members afflicted with Gulf War illnesses were taken care of. Like Kim, Mike coached Randy on not accepting the ridiculous thirty percent disability compensation the VA initially offered.

During the first few years of Randy's ALS fight, Mike watched as Randy's body slowly deteriorated. He was unsure how he could help. Then, in May 1995, Mike experienced a radical conversion through a relatively new men's evangelical Christian organization called Promise Keepers.

chapter twenty-four

PROMISE KEEPER

"I looked for a man among them who would build up a wall and stand before me in the gap."

Ezekiel 22:30 (NIV)

As a member of this, "Christ-centered organization dedicated to introducing men to Jesus Christ as their Savior and Lord and helping them to grow as Christians," Mike was turned on to faith and shared it with everyone.

In 1995, he first experienced the word of God while at a PK event in Washington D.C.'s RFK Stadium. Standing down on the field close to the keynote speaker, Reverend Jack Williams Hayford, internationally acclaimed author and Pentecostal minister, Mike suddenly felt the need to forgive himself by, "Taking a step into forgiveness." Something unusual was about to happen in Mike's life. For some reason, unknown at the time, the Holy Spirit told Mike to, "Tell the Chaplain of the Senate that he had forgiven himself."

Mike shared that he didn't even know there was a Chaplain of the Senate but the next day attempted to contact him. Twice he tried calling not realizing the Senate was in recess. Finally, his call was answered. After explaining the purpose of his call, Mike listened intently as the woman said, "I've never heard this one before." Nonetheless, she advised Mike to come to the Senate the next week and the Chaplain would meet him. During the next year and a half, the Senate Chaplain mentored Mike on his personal religious journey which leads to our next story.

As Randy watched his once athletic body waste away, of course he questioned, "Why?" Good friends, family, medical experts, and spiritual leaders offered comfort and explanation to the best of their abilities. Randy searched for his purpose which manifested itself two years later at another Promise Keeper event.

Within the shadows of monuments to great American leaders, on a hot, humid October 1997 day, more than a million men swarmed the Washington Mall to share spiritual unity. Searching for a miracle or human cure, Randy decided he had to make this journey. So, he and his family loaded up the conversion van and drove the eight-hour trip from Emerald Isle to Washington.

While his family joined Lisa in D.C., Randy and his dad accompanied Mike and Mike's father to the *men's only* day-long session on the Mall.

Heberts and Brahams visit Washington, D. C.

"Standing in The Gap" 1997

Arriving early, the foursome pushed as close as possible, stopping half a Mall away near the Smithsonian Air and Space Museum. Other men had been arriving from across the world for days; flying, driving, and some even walking to the Capitol. Tents, teepees, and flags representing individuals' states were scattered about the Mall -- people kept coming, and coming, and coming. It looked like a religious Woodstock.

As the morning grew into afternoon and the autumn sun found its zenith across clear and sunny skies, the temperature soared. With very little breeze squeezing between the mass of men, it was, as Mike remembered, "Hot as sin." Even so, men were singing and hugging and presenters were blaring messages about their, "A Sacred Assembly of Men," theme on six jumbotron screens. C-Span and other televisions stations provided live coverage as, accompanied by a chorus and full orchestra, men were urged to "Stand in The Gap" in a day of personal repentance and prayer. Bill McCartney, former University of Colorado football head coach and Promise Keeper founder, urged the men to, "Take the spirit of unity back home…"

In an excited swaying frenzy, Evangelicals waved their hands in the air while more subdued Christians waited patiently for the keynote speaker. Finally, he asked everyone to raise their hands to pray. Mike asked Randy if he could.

Randy said, "Yes" and cried as Mike and he asked for forgiveness of their sins. Soon thereafter the men were encouraged to assume a prostrate position on the grass in deep reverence for God! Rarely is our Capitol so quiet as to "hear" nearly 1.3 million men lying on the ground praying in total silence for what seemed to be hours. "This was a most amazing moment to share with Randy," Mike recalled. Eventually the presenters returned to their rhetoric and Randy communicated he had to pee. As we know, life goes on and Mike found himself escorting Randy to a sweltering booney in the middle of the Mall helping him go to the bathroom.

While they didn't get their miracle on the Mall in October, they did share a glorious experience with their earthly dads and Heavenly Father, mending relationships that needed attention, and as Mike put it, "Worshiping God in the presence of his conduit, a man named Randy." Mike summed up his close relationship with Randy as, "Having a friend with an inside track to the big man."

chapter twenty-five

THE ISLAND OF PATMOS MEDALLION

"Within the covers of the Bible are the answers for all the problems men face."

President Ronald Reagan

Randy's father, Loyd Hebert, is a unique man. A brilliant mind, at times he seems to be well ahead of the conversation, such as the time Mike walked in while visiting Randy. Mike recounted an interesting experience:

Randy's dad who was also visiting said to Mike, "When you walked in, the Holy Spirit said to me, 'You're the one!'"

Mike told me, "I wasn't sure what he was even talking about."

In a moment, Randy's father adamantly continued saying forcefully, "I heard Him three times and He says, "You're the one!""

Mike was still mystified. So was Randy.

Randy's father continued, explaining that when he traveled to the Island of Patmos, an Aegean island in the north of Greece's Dodecanese island group, where St. John, the Theologian, is said to have written the Book of Revelations, he was told to buy a medallion at a nun's trinket stand. She told him he would know who to give it to when the time was right. He added, "This island is a "significant Christian pilgrimage site" because of its proximity to the apocalyptic conclusion of the New Testament."

The Medallion

As a devout Christian, Loyd bought the medallion and waited for years to give it to the right person. He had no idea how important Christ had become in Mike's life as a Promise Keeper and insisted that he accept the medallion, restating that the Holy Spirit said, "You're the one." Mike continues to cherish this *sign,* believing it to be from God, wondering what the next will be, and knowing he had a part in strengthening Randy's walk with Christ.

chapter twenty-six

SHALLOW BREATHS

"The wisest one-word sentence? Breathe."

Terri Guillemets

An earlier example that tested Randy and his walk with God occurred soon after the family moved back into their remodeled house. Beginning their second decade with ALS, Randy and Kim were adjusting to as normal a routine as possible. Kim often woke at five a.m. and went for a power walk before Randy woke up. This was a great way to release pent up worries and steel herself for the next day.

One early June morning Kim quietly left for her walk leaving the rest of the family asleep. On this day Randy woke early and could hear their little dog Cindy moving restlessly on Kim's bed. During the early days Randy didn't have to sleep with his eyes taped so he could see the dog moving about. His fear was that the dog might jump onto his bed and dislodge his trach tubing.

As Randy's mind began to race, so did his heart rate. Randy reminded himself that *he should trust in God; that everything would be okay*. Like anyone would be, he was still scared.

Praying was something Randy was comfortable doing and since he didn't know when Kim would be back he started praying for God to keep him calm and relaxed. Quickly he felt God's presence.

He also sensed the presence of Cindy as she had indeed hopped off the bed. *Where was she going?*

Randy mentally prepared for the next jump which he knew would be on his bed – it was.

Randy thought, *I am not ready to die* and suddenly the peace of the Lord came over him. Even though Cindy had begun to scratch directly on the hose attached to the trach, Randy trusted in the Lord. She continued scratching the hose connection at the bottom – if that came off, Randy's airway would be blocked and he would suffocate.

Sure enough, Cindy scratched the hose once more and it came off, miraculously at the top, not the bottom.

Randy waited for the alarm to sound which he knew would be in about fifteen seconds. The ventilator no longer delivered the eleven breaths per minute Randy needed to live. To top this off, Cindy innocently laid across Randy's chest and the disconnected hose. Time seemed to move slowly but eventually Randy was able to take short shallow breaths. He was getting as few as two breaths per minute. Then, that same calming effect, a coolness across his entire body, again reminded Randy to trust in God.

Randy laid there for the next half hour relying on two shallow breaths per minute while his unknowing dog stayed there, unable to help.

Finally finished exercising, Kim's footsteps were a welcome sound as she bounded up the stairs. Hearing the alarming ventilator as she entered through the back door, Kim had raced upstairs and quickly reattached the hose. Needless to say, that ended her early morning walks.

Without the power of prayer and faith in God's purpose for him, Randy might not have survived while only receiving twenty percent of the necessary oxygen for thirty minutes.

Would you?

chapter twenty-seven

LIGHT AS A FEATHER

**"HOPE IS THE THING WITH FEATHERS
THAT PERCHES IN THE SOUL"**

Emily Dickinson

Throughout the better part of three decades Randy and Kim have been public role models while they have quietly endured their own personal demons. Kim shared how her life seemingly morphed overnight from wife to caregiver. New obstacles appeared daily. She once said, "…literally had to shake off the proverbial devil on my shoulder every day."

Many times, Randy and Kim struggled under the sheer weight of physical and mental challenges that come with living with ALS. Questions including *have we done enough, why me, am I up to this task, will I ever get to sleep again*, as well as *will I ever get over being angry* used to be commonplace. Even experienced healthcare providers and caregivers struggle with these issues as they maneuver through the process of long term illness or from patient to patient.

Other than a deep relationship with God, patience and hope may be the most important virtues when assisting long term care patients.

Having an empathetic attitude makes it so much easier to help. But sometimes, attitude just won't get it done. In fact, the dead-weight of these patients can cause physical harm to them as well as caregivers. Kim shared one such example that reinforces the importance of trusting in God's power.

In 1997, Kim was caring for two toddlers who didn't sleep much and Randy who also struggled with sleep. Kim struggled too…with sleep deprivation. While the kids would often cry themselves back to sleep, Randy was unable – ALS was taking over. Randy had lost control of his arms and could no longer stand on his own. His breathing had become labored. Restless nights were becoming the norm and Kim *dreamed* about getting just one good night's sleep.

One evening, after the kids went to bed easily, Kim also got Randy settled down for the night. Finally, she was going to get some sleep!

It didn't last long.

Soon after Kim fell asleep, Randy woke her. While Kim was completely exhausted, Randy couldn't breathe. Kim got up and tried for over an hour to get him physically comfortable. Nothing seemed to help and Randy insisted he wanted to get up. Like any couple disagreeing at two a.m. they argued. Kim was simply too tired and exhausted to move Randy or argue. Eventually Kim knew she had to relent.

By now Kim had become quite adept in helping Randy transfer to his wheelchair and got him to sit at the edge of the bed. But with Randy unable to assist and perhaps because of Kim's exhaustion, he slid to the floor. Kim immediately realized she was in big trouble. Randy was a big guy to begin with and his dead weight made it even more unlikely that Kim could get him back into the bed. Trying would likely injure them both and Kim did not want to call for help this early in the morning.

After fruitlessly trying for thirty minutes, Kim realized she could never lift Randy by herself so she put a pillow under his head to make him comfortable.

For some reason Kim had not remembered the power of prayer. When she did it hit her hard. Loudly she exclaimed to Randy, "Wait! We have to pray about this Randy!"

After soulfully praying for God's assistance, Kim looked at Randy and said, "Okay Randy, we're going to do this. On the count of three…one, two, three."

Kim lifted Randy.

She told me, "I don't recall feeling Randy at all. It was like he floated back into the bed. She looked at him and said, "I didn't lift you!"

The answered prayer was real! Light as a feather, God heard Kim's prayers and lifted the challenge of Randy's dead-weight. The struggle was real. The lift was real! God's power *is* real!

Thomas P. Gill

part four

HERSTORY

chapter twenty-eight

ANSWERED PRAYER

"To be a Christian without prayer is no more possible than to be alive without breathing."

Martin Luther

Many people have commented over the past twenty some years, "Kim must be an angel." Where other spouses may have left when the ALS or otherwise stricken patient deteriorated, Kim only became stronger. Of course, she has her ups and downs – that's natural. Like Randy, Kim has remained faithful to the wedding vows she took at Camp Lejeune – 'til death do us part! Then again, she, nor Randy had any idea what was in store for them, much like all of us.

Shortly after getting married and having their first child, Nicole, the Marine Corps transferred the young family to Missouri. Randy was already ALS symptomatic – he just didn't know he was ill. And, during the ensuing twelve months their lives would change, forever. Kyle was already in the womb and joined the family just thirteen months after Nicole. Thankfully the Marine Corps, through Smitty, ensured they were relocated to the East Coast where Randy would be closer to family and more advanced medical facilities in Bethesda, Maryland.

Imagine now as Randy's health is declining. The two babies are growing! What it must have been like as Kim is learning to take care of two babies while her husband is struggling to continue walking and feeding himself? The normal paradigm of helping newborns and toddlers learn skills was turned on its head. As the days move into weeks; weeks turn into months; and finally, months roll into years, Randy couldn't physically do as much as he would like. He couldn't walk, couldn't hold his adorable wife and beautiful children, and eventually required a tracheotomy to ensure his failing breathing muscles wouldn't prevent him from suffocating. Meals become a liquid shake through a feeding tube. The kids grew out of diapers and learned to eat and walk as Randy moved in the opposite direction.

With the clock ticking, the paradigm shift continued as Kim also learned how to ensure the Veterans Administration would continue taking care of her husband's medical needs, worked with the nurse staffing company to hire, train, and retain the staff (which Randy continues to do even now), ensured their house remains a "home" and does not become a health care center, and so much more. All along, Kim also hoped to ensure their friends didn't abandon them, as often happens with chronic or terminal illnesses, remained in good health and fitness to care for the family, tirelessly fought to ensure Randy and she maintain a husband/wife and father/mother relationships and their sanity, and devoted countless hours to raise money and awareness for the ALS Foundation. As you imagine these challenges in your mind's eye, read how Kim successfully accomplished them and if you listen closely you might even hear the beautiful melody of the late John Lennon's "Imagine."

Kim imagined how this life was going to change during the first year. As Randy declined in health, she moved back and forth through the emotional grief stages. Selflessly, but quietly, crying and lamenting the loss of her beautiful husband while at the same time loving and adoring her beautiful children, Kim struggled. Who wouldn't?

One day, during the early years, something truly divine happened to give Kim peace and inspire her to write the following message entitled *Answered Prayer* for their Chapel by the Sea newsletter which ultimately thanked Randy.

"Have you ever just prayed, and prayed and waited and waited for an answer? Have you wished as I have that God would just appear to give you His answer? I'm sure you have and all of us have even wondered if He heard us to begin with. This past month I prayed, and God answered in a way that I couldn't pass up this opportunity to share with you."

"During the past three months, Randy has experienced another dramatic stage of his Amyotrophic Lateral Sclerosis (ALS). He is now dependent on a ventilator full-time. Getting to this stage brought on a three-month mental ordeal for Randy as he fought fear, depression, insomnia, anxiety and stress. Our whole day was centered on comforting Randy, praying and assuring him God was with him. His nurse and I prayed with him, friends prayed, Clay (Pastor Clay) made special trips to assure him, but nothing seemed to help."

Kim added this during an interview years later, "This new challenge, not breathing for himself, was scary and one more loss that Randy was going to have to get used to. It was giving in to ALS.

The message continued,

"One morning, after an awful night, I arose just in time to open the door for the nurse. I begged for a few minutes in hopes that a cup of coffee would open my eyes. As I began to head downstairs, a verse came into my head, "Though I walk through the valley of death, I shall fear no evil." (Psalm 23). I questioned this as I said this to myself for a second time. What does "shadow" of death mean? Death is light, not darkness! This puzzled me, but I went about getting my coffee. I headed upstairs to begin my normal routine."

"The phone rang. It was my friend Elizabeth Geiger. She said, 'Kim, I'm coming over right now!'"

"Okay," I replied.

"The nurse took over and I headed downstairs and grabbed another cup of coffee. As soon as I had one sip, Elizabeth walked in with her Bible in her hand. She sat down and opened her Bible and said, 'I have something to share with you.' Elizabeth began to read, 'Though I walk through the valley of the shadow of death, I shall fear no evil for thou art with me...' *My body froze, the hair on my arms and head stood straight up, and I had goose bumps all over my body.* She continued, 'and I'm here to explain what the shadow of death means.'"

"That instant I felt myself leave my body and I asked her to pinch me, because I knew I was dreaming. I told her what had just happened before she called and Elizabeth calmly replied that it was all God's plan. Once again, she amazed me with her faith."

"You see, God placed Elizabeth the night before in a Bible study where they studied the meaning of the shadow of death. The shadow of death means that, before God gave us Christ, we feared death. Jesus died for us and rose from the dead to comfort us and confirm to us we have life after death and we need not fear for He will always be with us. I couldn't believe it. God answered me through Elizabeth."

"I rushed upstairs to share the news with Randy. It was only then that I knew the message was for Randy's benefit, not mine. God was passing a simple message along through a Bible study, to Elizabeth, to me, just to get to Randy, *"FEAR NOT RANDY, FOR I AM WITH YOU."*

"An incredible warmth filled the room as I realized God had been in that room every morning for the past three months listening, and now He was answering Randy."

"Randy," I said, "He is telling you He is with you.'"

"Wow! How powerful is that! I can't begin to explain or express to you the overwhelming feeling I had through this experience. It was so incredible, I was left in awe for weeks."

"Never again will I ask or wonder if God is listening. I have had a confirmation from the Lord Himself, He hears all prayers. It is Randy's illness that led me to the Lord and he has changed my life in ways that I could never have imagined. He has taught me many lessons of love, patience, perseverance and character, but mostly, He has taught me how faith can get you through anything."

"Thank you, Randy, for giving me the best gift of love ever, Jesus Christ."

"Love, Kim Hebert"

chapter twenty-nine

MARINE WIFE: ANGEL OR CHAMELEON

"God promises to make something good out of the storms that bring devastation to your life."

Romans 8:28

It would be great to say after having her prayer answered life had been all roses. That would be a far cry from the truth as everyone involved in Randy's life are human beings. Remembering God is with us and has a master plan helps each of us get through the struggles of constant change and worries like infections and other life altering issues.

Life altering issues. What are they? In Kim's case they began with Randy telling her that he was ill and providing her a pamphlet to read about ALS. As a Marine and *man's man* Randy had been masking his concerns about his illness until he knew all the answers. By then, they were a family of four and needing a lot of help. After Randy's boss helped them get back to Camp Lejeune, Kim settled into their *new normal* as she watched Randy decline. Some have described her in this role as chameleon-like, easily adaptable and capable of moving from challenge to challenge, not unlike Ms. Maudie described by Scout in *To*

Kill a Mockingbird. Or, perhaps she is a Marine wife.

One of her primary duties in addition to raising her two toddlers was caring for Randy. In the beginning there was zero nursing assistance. The Marine Corps offered Randy a seventy percent disability medical retirement which he did not accept. Knowing this was a terminal illness potentially requiring long term care Randy requested a formal medical board make a decision on this disability recommendation. The board met and prior to Randy even entering the room to hear the decision they had raised it to one hundred percent. However, Randy told them, "I drove six hours to get here and want to be heard." He then proceeded to share his story of being exposed to chemicals on behalf of the countless others who had been contaminated.

Kim constantly wrote beseeching VA officials at all levels, including physicians and administrators, to increase the hours of care Randy was entitled to. Prior to Randy's congressional hearing testimony in 1996, Kim received only two hours of nursing help **per week**. Following the testimony in which Randy's dad and Kim assisted in telling his story, the Marine Corps Commandant, Four Star General Charles Krulak, met with and assured them that they would be taken care of immediately. They were. General Krulak cut the red tape and ensured Randy was quickly retired with a one hundred percent rating in the VA system in thirty days. This is an outstanding example of a Marine taking care of his own.

Kim continues to work with the VA urging for improved care of all ALS and Gulf War Syndrome patients. Tim Rogers, CEO of the Association for Home and Hospice Care of North Carolina and the South Carolina Home Care Association, perhaps said it best, "… what really sets Kim apart is her unbridled commitment to ensure all American veterans afflicted with ALS, not just her husband, are cared for and not forgotten."

Creating these ripples of healthcare awareness could be a full-time job itself notwithstanding caring for Randy. Additionally, Kim works closely with Randy in hiring all his nursing care. Not all patients would want to do this, but physicians I spoke with about Randy's decades of unique longevity suggest that this may be due in part to Kim and Randy's direct involvement in hiring, training, and managing the nursing staff at their home. Keep in mind Kim has fought to ensure her home remains absent of the unneeded medical equipment, antiseptic smells that usually permeate clinics, and nursing scrubs. The required medical equipment is present but Kim insists that their house is a *home* first and foremost.

In addition to being a pseudo clinic manager for more than two decades, Kim continues to be a remarkable host for visitors. A fantastic cook, everyone is adamant about the delicious food Kim prepares for them in her beautifully stocked kitchen. And it's not just the food or presentation! Kim finds time to give back to multiple charities throughout the year. Once, when talking with Randy, we had to relocate to another room because the twelve-foot long kitchen table was covered with forty vases that Kim was preparing for a gala supporting the Coastal Pregnancy Care Center annual charity drive.

Kim is the first to say God has blessed her life and surrounded her with many great family and friends. But during this time in which, "One minute I was on top of the world – married to a handsome Marine Captain with two beautiful babies - the next day he came home with ALS," she has also endured the tragedy of losing both of her loving parents in a few short years. Perhaps Kim again questioned her faith after her physically fit father died unexpectedly and soon after her mother died in an automobile crash just outside her neighborhood. Bluntly, she told me, "I struggled with the loss of my parents and it took months for me to focus. I couldn't hide in my bed and cry. I still had a job to do."

Even still, Kim firmly believes as Randy told me, "God doesn't make mistakes!" Her girlfriends and brother showered Kim with love and helped her cope with these losses allowing her to continue to care for Randy. These loving friends are such a diverse group of women you might only find on Emerald Isle.

The common theme among these friends is, "Kim is an Angel on Earth!" Many people I spoke with honestly question whether they would have stayed in their relationship if their spouse had ALS. For Kim, that wasn't even a question; wife, caregiver, mother, friend, charity supporter, and above all, Christian. That's what matters! Friends and of course her brother and sisters would do anything for Kim, as she will for them.

There are countless examples but one that came to mind while preparing this chapter is how Kim observed a neighbor laying pine straw in the heat of the day. Kim stopped what she was doing, walked right over, and helped her finish the task – without asking. That is who she is!

Another prominent theme running deep through most conversations is how Randy and Kim maintain the traditional mom and dad relationships, including decision making and disciplinary focus. "Go ask Dad," might be Kim's response or direction to the kids when they misbehaved or had a question. For the little ones to climb right up into Randy's lap would be as common as them suctioning his trach. Keep in mind, throughout this life style change to ensure Randy received the nursing care and the rest his bodily needs, much like a Cinderella princess, Kim has become a deliberate clock watcher, always cognizant of her nurses' schedules and needing to be home when they are not available.

As Kim received VA approval for enhanced nursing care, she got a little bit of respite although she never really stops thinking about Randy. In the mornings she wakes up knowing that in a few minutes at least one caregiver will be in her bedroom helping to ready Randy for the new day. Her life has been about service – not servant – to ensure Randy receives the best life and care possible. Perhaps this is what true love and devotion look like. Sometimes the traditional roles just won't work when one is physically challenged. Believing in oneself and trusting in God, while knowing that you just have to get it done, is all you need. Take for example one afternoon when neighbor Charlie stopped by for a quick visit.

Charlie said, "It was hotter than four hells and the elevator was broken." On a summer weekend at the beach it is unlikely to get any repairman, much less someone who works on elevators, to dispatch quickly. Kim had already done what any *sane* wife would do. She took her tools, squeezed into the dark, dank elevator shaft, and using a flashlight, located the problem. This is where Charlie found her. Sweaty and dirty, Kim was a mess. But she wasn't complaining – "just fixing the elevator." The cable had slid off its track with Randy and the young kids in the elevator. While Nicole and Kyle kept Randy company, Kim pried the elevator door open and jumped into the shaft to fix it.

No bigger than a minute, Kim was using her full weight and a pry bar to try to move the cable. In the foul, oxygen deprived, cramped space, Charlie took shallow breaths as he helped Kim successfully get the cable on the track. Thinking back on this experience Charlie exclaimed, "Kim is the hardest working woman I've ever known."

As a health care supporter, Kim is a tireless spouse who has gone head to head with bureaucrats and administrators at all levels of the government and hospitals. Kim believes that "no" means "let me speak with your supervisor" until she gets the right answer. Ensuring only the best care for Randy has been front and center. David Dorworth said, "Kim never whines, complains or gives up; she had a sixth sense of fighting bureaucracy to win the battle with the Department of Defense." Perhaps Kim was born with this, or perhaps like a mama "A Bear" she has learned this skill to ensure her husband is treated fairly. Kim's tenacious attitude and effort has paid off as the care for Randy and other veteran ALS patients continues to improve. It is just this drive and protective nature that resulted in Kim being honored several times by the ALS Association and other healthcare groups including being the recipient of the 2006 National Association for Home Care & Hospice Clara Barton Caregiver of the Year.

2006 National Caregiver of the Year

Kim responded to this personal acclaim with humility adding, "The Lord has kept my husband alive for twelve years with this illness. He's not only kept him alive, but He's kept him with a good spirit and attitude which made it easy for me and my children to be able to handle this disease. Another blessing is that He surrounded us with many rich friendships that help us through every day; and one more blessing is that He provided us with a home care agency that has compassion."

Kim continued, saying about her agency, "…you have personally come to my home and met my family. You understand our needs, you put a face to my family so we know who you are – but *you also know who we are*, and what our needs are. … sent women to our house that have faith as we do and compassion. You can have all the technical skills, but if you don't have the compassion with the technical skills, then you're lacking something. And families, like ours really need everything; we need the technical skills with the compassion."

Ironically, when Kim was recognized as the National Caregiver of the Year the hotel did not provide a handicap accessible room. That did not deter Kim but did make her very angry. Given the reason they were there they were still unsuccessful in getting a different room after trying for an hour. So, they improvised like every good Marine and spouse.

Kim simply moved the room's furniture around, both got bathed, and were ready to go to the awards ceremony after a grueling day caravanning to Baltimore. Late that evening Kim and Randy followed Charlie and Dorla as they drove back to Emerald Isle not realizing that the nearby NFL Ravens and Redskins game had also just finished. What should have taken seven, took eleven hours of difficult driving to ensure Randy was safe and comfortable in his own surroundings.

During my year-long encounters with Randy and Kim, I observed first-hand as both continue to fight for what is rightfully theirs and other patients. As recently as early 2017 Kim was urging the VA to provide extended evening coverage which would improve their quality of life. North Carolina Congressman Walter B. Jones is Kim's hero as he twice helped Kim get the VA to extend Randy's nursing coverage. As Kim has referred to herself and the nursing staff as Randy's "privates" she initially helped train the new staff into what is now a finely tuned healthcare regimen. It wasn't always like that, as Kim, Randy, and friends will attest. After nearly twenty-five years they have this process down to a science. "He knows what's good for him and we pretty much do what Randy wants us to do," Kim replies when asked how she helps Randy.

In addition to pushing for improved quality care for Randy and others, Kim was an aggressive community activist getting the Bogue Banks townships to improve handicap accessibility to the beach. Kim and the Mayor's Committee for Disabilities took the initiative to photograph every access on the twenty-mile-long island and met with local leaders describing in detail what they lacked in public handicap beach access. Current Emerald Isle Town Manager Frank Rush recently shared how, "Kim was directly responsible for ensuring how the beach towns think about and act on modifying access ramps." In addition to refurbishing plans for Randy's Way, Emerald Isle, like Jetton Pier on another North Carolina barrier island, is experimenting with movable extension mats to ensure beach goers needing additional mobility help can get closer to the water. Emerald Isle's beautiful Eastern and Western public access ramps are superior and are the result of Kim's fighting for her husband and all physically challenged beach lovers.

"Mother." What does that term really mean? One definition shares, "…selfless, loving human who must sacrifice many of their wants and needs for the wants and needs of their children." In the Hebert case, as in countless others around the world, this can also mean sacrificing for their husband. And to be fair, it could be just the opposite given that ALS and other serious life challenges are non-discriminating relative to traditional sex norms. It's just that, well, we expect a different type of comfort and caring from a woman and a mom. And Kim delivers. She continues to orchestrate the family schedules as she has for the past two decades ensuring at least one parent has been at every one of Nicole's and Kyle's special school, sports, church, or other extracurricular events. When possible, it was both parents.

When Randy was hospitalized in May 2017 at the Durham VA hospital for three weeks, Kim raced back and forth on Interstate 40, a round trip of more than three hundred miles, to ensure she could help celebrate Kyle's UNC Wilmington college graduation, while also being back with Randy as soon as possible. While she will tell you their dedicated and heroic nurses left their homes and stayed with Randy so she could participate, Kim is the person who committed to being in both places and drove back and forth on the highway. Another hero is sister Robin who left her home in Rocky Mount, drove to Durham, and picked up Kim for the drive back to Wilmington. Of course, Kim facetimed with Randy in his hospital bed so he could watch Kyle graduate.

The stork didn't just drop off the kids ready to go to college as the aforementioned might imply. Like every other family, there were all the newborn experiences such as falling and learning to walk while simultaneously their father was trying to continue to stand and walk. There were utensils to learn how to use and foods to learn how to eat as Randy was learning how to consume different foods that would not cause him to aspirate. These were eventually replaced by a feeding tube. Consider this: as both infants moved into being toddlers Randy was moving in the opposite direction so that at one-point Kim was taking care of three human beings experiencing new learning situations daily – with almost no help other than what family and friends provided.

There are plenty of current day examples of moms who raise multiple young children and of course some who also care for a chronically and or terminally ill spouse or other family member in the home. I am not suggesting that Kim is a unique mother. It is her character and how she dealt with this unique situation that is special. As her small family required more and more of her attention, Kim provided it, learning how to help care for Randy, Nicole and Kyle at the same time.

While Randy could still travel, Kim ensured the kids were afforded as many experiences as possible including loading everyone up and driving to Disney. Friends like Annita and Henry joined them and remembered how much Randy and the kids enjoyed this trip. Speaking of the kids, Kyle said Nicole is, "…literally one of my best friends." Nicole shared similar thoughts when I met her at their beach house this summer. Grounded, thoughtful and compassionate young adults, Kyle is completing a master's degree through UNC Wilmington and Nicole is working as a Recreational Therapist in Boulder, Colorado. Kyle is an accomplished world-wide surfer, teaches surfing, and gives kayak tours on the island during the summer.

Nicole offered two of her favorite and most cherished mementoes which are letters her dad "wrote" to her. Both show, "How thoughtful and loving my dad is." Nicole shared how she also loves to lay out on the "concrete beach" with her dad. One recent memory is when she and Randy discussed a book on leadership, faith, and finding purpose in life. "Something about sitting with Dad and reading that book helped me overcome so much and helped me become motivated in this new way."

Both children love their mom and dad without question and have multiple *best friends*, not unlike Randy and Kim. Kyle summed up his childhood as, "I've lived a good life and had a blessed childhood."

Nicole (8) and Kyle (7) kissing Dad

One memory Randy holds dear is when Kyle and Nicole colored with ink pens on their beautiful leather sectional.

"Now remember, I can't move or even grunt for them to stop, and well, when they were just about four and three years old, Kim was upstairs and I guess I was "watching the kids." At the time, Kim was my primary caregiver in addition to mom and wife.

When Kim came down stairs, Nicole and Kyle had drawn beautiful smiley faces all over our couch – it could have been much worse. I still remember the kids sitting on the edge of the fireplace with instructions to *not say a word.* Of course, I couldn't either. Kim was really mad and chewed the kids out while she tried to clean the couch. Thankfully she was able to remove the ink.

Fifteen minutes later, as she cleaned the couch, Kim realized she did not hear the kids. Screaming, Kim frantically searched everywhere. Soon, a good friend, Suzanne, called saying she had both kids and was bringing them home. Nicole explained that she and Kyle had packed their underwear and were walking down narrow Coast Guard Road to move to Miss Annita's house because, "She is nicer than Mom."

The youngsters couldn't comprehend exactly how much "Mom" was having to do just to keep their heads above water.

Another favorite memory is the Mexican send-off *Mom* hosted, attended by over one hundred friends, when Nicole moved cross-country to Denver to begin her recreational therapist career. Certainly, a strong mom and devoted dad are essential ingredients for these successful young adults and loving children.

Kim has well delivered on the "Better or worse" vow and Randy knows it well! As a loving and caring wife, she has remained faithfully by his side. Even when afforded respite trips with her girlfriends, she always checks in with Randy. Each of her friends individually recounted how Kim will call home several times during the day to check on Randy to see how his day is going.

Likewise, Randy has honored his wife and as a husband ensured she knows how much he appreciates what she does for him. Confined to a wheelchair, Randy still dotes on his bride. One touching example is how he faithfully sends roses on all special occasions as he has done since they married in 1992. Then again, he does think he lives with an angel.

***

"God could not be everywhere, and therefore he made mothers."

Rudyard Kipling

chapter thirty

ANGELS AMONGST US

"I've seen and met angels wearing the disguise of ordinary people living ordinary lives."

Tracy Chapman

Just five years into their ALS journey, when Nicole was five and Kyle was four, Kim penned the following words:

"If I had a quarter for every time someone asked me, "How do you do what you do?" I think my cup would "runneth over" a thousand times. I hope my response to you is well heard, and not taken lightly, because it truly is the grace of God that lightens my load."

"I always thought I was the type who couldn't handle stress. I truly depended upon Randy for his strength and wisdom to calm me down. Now, through Randy's illness, I have become more aware and more dependent upon a greater strength--the Lord's strength."

"There are so many times I have felt His presence right beside me. I have felt His hands lift Randy when I knew I didn't have an ounce of strength left. I have felt Him take the burden of pain from my heart when I thought I could not take any more. I have felt Him shower me with love and strength when all I felt was anger and despair. I have seen God's work all around me, and it is amazing how much He has done just for me."

"The most incredible gift that God has given me is the love that He surrounds my family with! So many of His angels have come to my rescue when I let my guard down. When I am at the lowest point, it never fails, God sends His servants my way, either by phone, letter or in person. Yes, I have actually been frightened by how His timing is so perfect and precise. It is not only amazing how He sent his angels to be by my side, but how His earthly "angels" didn't hesitate to respond to the calling that God placed on them. My breath is taken from me, and I think, what faithful followers of the Lord!"

"I want to thank you "earthly angels" for helping my family through this trial we face. You have made it easier with all your prayers and all your love."

"If you have any doubt that maybe you couldn't do, remember when facing a hardship, illness or death, God surely will take your hand, He will never leave or forsake you. The stronger your faith, the lighter the load."

"If I left you wondering about angels, the next time you are in church look around you, because the "angels are amongst us!""

Nineteen years after being written, nothing in these words has changed, although the author would add that Kim is an Angel Amongst Us.

***

"Believers look up—take courage. The angels are nearer than you think."

Billy Graham

part five
RIPPLES OF HEALTH CARE

RIPPLES OF HEALTH CARE

**"If I had six hours to chop down a tree, I'd
spend the first four hours sharpening the axe."**

Abraham Lincoln

Once in a lifetime, maybe twice if one is
fortunate, a person gets to participate in something
that will perhaps be a legacy moment. In Randy's
case, obviously this moment is surviving ALS.

Or, is it?

Like another military hero, Air Force Major
Michael Donnelly, who succumbed to ALS after a
few short years, Randy has trumpeted the need for
continued investigation, research, improved
diagnosis and prognosis, and communication to all
stake holders on all war illnesses, not just Gulf
War Illnesses. Michael, and his father, Tom
Donnelly, led the charge in testifying before
congressional hearings and in raising the
awareness of the unusually high number of combat
veterans afflicted with ALS. In the November 7,
1997 report entitled, Gulf War Veteran's Illnesses:
VA, DOD Continue to Resist Strong Evidence
Linking Toxic Causes to Chronic Health Effects.
Second Report by the Committee on Government
Reform and Oversight Together with Additional

Views, many readers were shocked at what the testifying veterans were sharing. As I mentioned earlier, what happened during the short war and following months were overshadowed at what apparently was an intentional disregard for the health and welfare of the military members and their families.

While Major Donnelly fought valiantly only to lose his fight with ALS, Randy continues to serve as a reminder to patients, family members, caregivers, and the entire medical community that there is hope. Ongoing ALS studies which the VA and Department of Defense are funding, along with American patriots like Ross Perot, and physicians Dr. Robert Haley and Duke's Dr. Richard Bedlack are providing evidence that like other diseases, there may eventually be a cure. The pebble tossed by Michael Donnelly followed by another and another and yet another offers all ALS patients and caregivers the one item that the opening of the proverbial Pandora's Box did not remove: HOPE! Now, there is hope as more and more veterans and their families receive the medical, psychological, educational, and home improvement service connected benefits they were denied for decades.

Nearly twenty years after the report was first published, Randy continues to provide VA physicians and other health care professionals a case study of desire, strength, and commitment as an advocate for others. Like the few other ALS patients who live decades with this disease, Randy is also providing an intimate look into what it takes to be a model patient. Randy and Kim would be quick to point out there have been times that Randy has been anything but a model patient.

One example is the early daily pity parties resulting in tearful months on end as he contemplated losing his last vestige of control; breathing on his own. Only after one of his loving caregivers whispered, "I received a message from our Loving Father; it's going to be alright," did Randy finally accept his tracheotomy. Before suffering this clinical *last straw*, Randy had endured numerous other medical challenges.

Getting a trach scared Randy more than anything. This invasive procedure would require him to use a ventilator for the rest of his life and was a bacterial infectious opportunity that could lead to pneumonia. By working closely with physicians and caregivers, Randy has limited his infections and complications, but there have been several dangerously close calls. Now, VA and Navy hospital doctors know if Randy *calls* they will almost always defer to his suggestions. They realize he has survived this long with ALS and he knows his body better than anyone.

As a patient, Randy has been willing to try many new and/or different suggestions, especially those that would allow him to communicate. With deteriorating muscle control and lack of voice, some of the typical devices were not effective. One example that was initially helpful was called EZ Keys. Before he lost all control of his legs, Randy could use a clicker button with his right leg to control his computer. Using this device, Randy assisted or guided good friends Dick Culp and Ed Johnson as they constructed a three hundred square foot medical storage supply area in his garage. Eventually, both legs failed and Randy resorted to the latest technologies such as eye gaze and a reflective sticker dot between his eyes. Desiring to remain in control, Randy tried desperately to engage them. Unfortunately, the calibration for both was difficult. He even tried the Computer Brain interface.

With a skull cap snuggly fitted on his head, several electrodes were secured to his scalp. It was timely and frankly painful as each hole had to be prepared with a gel and metal rod so the electrode would make contact. The entire set up took an hour, if lucky! Once it was ready, the computer had an alphabet board with lights under each letter. Randy's job was to concentrate on the letter he wanted the listener to know so he could spell out a word. Almost by magic, as the patient focused on a letter, the light would illuminate about thirteen times but each took about twenty seconds. Grueling, painful and inefficient -- Randy knew his process, designed by himself and his father and still in use today, is just the opposite.

Randy still communicates as he has for years. To the casual observer the process may seem difficult, but once practiced is pretty straight forward. To begin, a question is asked of Randy or he indicates he desires to communicate a thought. To get attention Randy simply stares at you. If one is not paying attention, for whatever reason, this could be a bit frustrating although one would never know it from chatting with Randy. To answer a question or provide a response to a comment, Randy simply listens to his caregiver, or other person, who quickly rattles off the alphabet such as "A, B, C, D…" When Randy hears the letter to the first word of his response, he moves his eyes in the direction of the caregiver who repeats the letter for clarification. Confirmed, they start with the second letter and then move on to the third and so forth. Once the first word is spelled out and the caregiver says it aloud, Randy will stare straight ahead to prepare for the second word…. I encourage all readers to try this at home but know that Randy, his nurses, and his family are such good listeners that sometimes they communicate faster and better than those of us with normal communication processes.

Sometimes not! There were more than a few times when the caregiver, Randy and I laughed as we could not figure out what in the world he was trying to say. Then, once we did, it was simple and exactly as it should have been. On more than one occasion Randy has had to *say* to the caregiver, "Stop Blowing Through the Alphabet" as they ABCed. I often wondered who has the communication challenge?

Other physical limitations for chronically or terminally ill patients include basic issues most people take for granted such as preparing for sleep and waking up.

Pretend for a moment that you can't move but really want to take a shower and go to bed. People without serious limitations can do this in ten minutes.

In Randy's case it can take as long as three hours. After the caregiver and or Kim takes Randy upstairs, they help him prepare for his shower. It typically requires two staff members to physically move Randy from the wheelchair to the shower and then they monitor the water for up to fifteen minutes to ensure it is the right temperature so Randy won't be scalded.

Sounds simple. I guarantee you it is not.

After drying every inch of this immobile, six-foot tall man, they transfer him back to the wheelchair to start the medical check-off list.

Once finished with the medical tasks, they ensure Randy is comfortable in his bed. This is critical as he can't easily communicate later should he need adjusted. Adequate sleep is very important, as is the proper positioning of Randy's body to alleviate the potential for bed sores. After several hours of preparation, Randy is settled and the caregiver is finished, unless Randy is ready to go to sleep. If so, his eyelids must be taped shut so they do not dry out at night as he cannot close them himself.

Okay, now it is time to go to sleep.

Fast forward about eight hours. As soon as Kim wakes up she walks over to Randy lying motionless in his bed and ensures he is okay. Most days, after un-taping his eyes, they talk about daily plans until nurses arrive. About seven a.m. the caregivers begin to reverse the evening routine. And what happens first? Randy offers that faint wisp of a smile as the corner of his mouth turns up and you know he is happy to be back in the world - ready for another day.

Randy and Kim have also tossed pebbles in the quasi-healthcare administrator pond as both have been instrumental in the hiring of the caregiving staff. "We know what Randy needs," Kim told me when I asked why they interview every potential nurse. "Taking care of Randy demands a special kind of focused individual," she continued and as I observed throughout my visits. While all the nurses have the basic education required to work with any patient, Randy provides an intense step-by-step training in communicating the "ABCs" as well as how to operate the wheelchair and associated components. Randy reviews the alarms, ventilator requirements, how to clean the trach and ventilator tube, and even how to provide his meals through the feeding tube. Randy expects his team to be alert, confident, patient, and willing to go with the flow. When I asked one of his nurses to describe this process she replied, "Randy is the most patient person I've ever met." Maybe this is another reason Randy has survived so long.

As I observed recently, Randy also helps ensure the staff knows how to order supplies and medicine from the VA hospital pharmacy. Red tape remains within most government agencies, yet Randy, Kim, and the staff work closely to ensure a seamless delivery of everything needed to keep Randy alive. While they were all too humble to take credit, we can only hope that they have had an impact on improving the delivery system for other long-term care veterans.

Not all the training and medical care is as smooth as it might sound from the previous paragraphs. I asked Randy to share some of his more memorable stories. Taken with a grain of salt, some of these could be hilarious while all could serve as teaching moments.

One of his nurses recounted how she used, as Randy said, "her baby brain" when she turned on the electric toothbrush before placing it into his mouth. Toothpaste was everywhere except his mouth! During training, another caregiver accidentally placed her foot on the wheelchair brake and couldn't get the extremely heavy chair to budge. Another staff member, providing coverage during the training, also had no idea what was wrong with the wheelchair. They carefully checked the battery and connections – no solution. Of course, Randy knew what was wrong and waited until they thought to ask him. He replied, "Read the screen... the brake is on." There were also stories of how Randy's legs would be bumped on walls by novice wheelchair drivers. Randy knew when it was about to happen but couldn't scream. His comment, "It doesn't hurt as much when you can't say anything." We could all learn from that comment.

The personnel hiring and training regimen is a well thought out process that has been successful over the past two decades. Being active in one's healthcare is an important life lesson. Yet, I believe the most telling aspect of Randy's personal healthcare management is that he thanks every caregiver every day when they take care of him – without fail!

Even when the patient is active and engaged, stuff happens! Having trained, competent, and attentive staff, along with a caring family is critical, such as we found in early summer of 2017. Panic attacks have been the norm for Randy due to many potential problems, but sometimes the real scares come from infection and/or having new staff members and physicians. During the early spring, Randy seemed to feel he had a sore lung which eventually sounded like he might have pneumonia. Graphically, his nurse reported that Randy's urine looked like sweet tea. During a routine dermatologist appointment on the same day, very important for someone who loves to tan, his physician suggested they complete additional lab work as Randy appeared a little "yellow." A phlebotomist tried to "stick" him numerous times to draw blood and eventually was successful getting a sample of blood from Randy's foot. He was absolutely jaundiced due to a problem with bile blockage. This began as series of admissions to several hospitals including the Camp Lejeune Naval Hospital, Carolina East Medical Center in New Bern, and the Durham, North Carolina Veterans Affairs hospital. Additional bloodwork and ultrasounds determined that Randy's gall bladder was chocked full of gall stones forming a severe and life-threatening blockage.

"What to do?" was the question as Randy really couldn't be placed under anesthesia or endure the necessary surgery to remove them. This is just another example of Randy and others leading the way for other patients and physicians to *practice* and determine best courses of actions. Back and forth from home to hospital, to other hospitals, and to specialists the process continued – the whole while Randy was critically ill. Other questions presented such as, "Was Randy in liver failure?" and "Would additional tests show if his blood was clotting adequately?" Failure to produce urine resulted in a subsequent admission to the nearby New Bern's Carolinas Medical Center East hospital on Randy's April 25th birthday, which finally resulted in the physicians surprisingly indicating Randy no longer had a stone blocking his bile duct. However, they still had questions such as should they remove the gall bladder or go home and see what happens.

Randy returned home on May 2nd, but the next day he had no urine output suggesting he was dehydrated. The next step was to travel nearly two hundred miles to the VA hospital where he got another medical opinion. Eventually, the doctors inserted a midline into Randy's arm, took a sputum sample, and diagnosed Randy with pneumonia. On May 4th, the midline was changed to a peripherally inserted central catheter or PICC line through his left arm as Randy settled into an expected longer stay. Surprisingly, the lab work came back better than expected and Randy was a *normal* (whatever that means) patient throughout the weekend. By Monday, as Randy's chemistries had continued to improve, he was discharged and went home.

For the next three weeks, Randy stayed in bed trying to recover and gain strength. He was, "wiped out!" On May 28th Randy finally felt well enough to have his first evening shower. He appeared to be on the mend, although panic attacks, caused by the hospitalizations, were frequent and resulted in a racing heart which required frequent "bagging" by his attendants or family. Dr. Bedlack, Randy's physician, authorized a new medicine to assist in decreasing the panic attacks. Finally, after eight weeks of a severe and unexpected health care twist, Randy started to recover. Yet, each recovery takes more and more out of him and they never know for sure what will be the next new challenge.

Long term care, such as described above, requires practicing patience which dictionaries define as, "The capacity to accept or tolerate daily, trouble or suffering, without getting angry or upset."

Kim once told me, "We all have different levels of anxiety, burdens or trials. The things that have kept my family grounded are faith, family and friends. My family has been blessed with countless compassionate people constantly keeping us motivated." Her message to others is, "If you are going through any life trials, look outside your box and see the gifts you may have around you. Faith, family and friends are there."

Whether you have help or not, are professionally trained, have an elderly patient, are a quadriplegic, mentally incapacitated, or one of many other possible challenges, long term care is hard work for the patient, caregivers, and family. Kim has served her role as mom, wife and caregiver with devotion and love where so many others might not have. Once more, this unique team has provided a wonderful example for others dealing with similar circumstances. One of the habits expressed in Stephen Covey's book, *Seven Habits of Highly Effective People,* is: "Sharpen the saw keeps you fresh so you can continue to practice the other six habits. You increase your capacity to produce and handle the challenges around you. Without this renewal, the body becomes weak, the mind mechanical, the emotions raw, the spirit insensitive, and the person selfish."

Without realizing she was serving as an example to others, Kim's continued quest for the VA to provide increased professional nursing coverage and respite care has ensured this availability for many others. With assistance from Congressman Walter B. Jones, Kim has been successful in getting the VA to increase daily nurse coverage to include Randy's waking up and bedtime routines while also allowing respite care. Remember, in the beginning, Kim had to perform all of these duties by herself. Kim can now *sharpen her saw* as she and Randy provide extraordinary examples of ripples within the healthcare pond!

Thomas P. Gill

part six
NEXT *"STEPS"*

NEXT *"STEPS"*

**"The journey of a thousand miles begins
with one step"**

Lao Tzu

I'm back to finish our journey and trust you enjoyed the first five sections. Collaborating with Tom on how to conclude this chapter of my life's story, we returned often to my next *steps* which is sort of an interesting concept for me, don't you agree? Then again, according to C.S. Lewis, a twentieth century author credited with thirty books including the Chronicles of Narnia series, "You are never too old to set another goal or to dream a new dream." A dear friend also says, "You are only as old as you feel." *Putting my best foot forward*, I think about one of my favorite people of all times, President Abraham Lincoln. His words hang prominently in our living room for all to embrace, "Live a good life. And in the end, it's not the years in your life that count, it's the life in your years."

For the past twenty-five years I have had to reset goals in part because so many people counted Kim and me out within a few years of my diagnosis. There are so many different paths that each of us could have taken but my primary goal initially was to honor my vows said before God to be faithful to my beautiful wife. Then I got ill and along came the kids -- we reset our goals. As I got sicker and they got bigger, my desires changed from being able to hold them to being able to see them play sports and graduate from high school. In a split second, as every parent will acknowledge, we were there, and reestablishing realistic goals despite what doctors were saying behind my back, and some to my face. Five years after Nicole finished high school, we now have two college graduates and Kyle is finishing his master's degree. What could possibly be our next goals?

Several objectives remain unchanged. First and foremost, I have a burning desire to be with my Lord and Savior. I am so thankful to God for allowing me the opportunity to enjoy the lives of so many family and friends and to be able to share our stories with so many others as a beacon for all to see that through Him all things are possible. Secondly, I intend to remain dedicated, faithful, and loving to my wife as she has enabled me to accomplish every goal we attempted. My heart breaks as I wrestle with the expectation that I will leave her on earth; at the same time, I know when I move on I will be with God and my family will join me at the appointed time. I also know God has provided for them in spiritual and earthly ways. So, if everything is taken care of, what then are my next steps?

Evidenced in this reflection of my life, I hope to lead many people to a lasting relationship with God. Perhaps those who already enjoy this blessing will have their religious saws sharpened and remember to share with others the rewards of walking with God and knowing the love He has for each of us. In John 8:12, Jesus spoke to the people saying, "I am the light of the world. If you follow me, you won't have to walk in darkness, because you will have the light that leads to life."

As an active healthcare participant -- not patient and not victim -- I want to continue to serve as a ripple of hope encouraging others with medical, physical, socioeconomic, psychiatric, or other challenges, to fight for what is right; to push the limit; to live on the edge; and to burst through the glass ceiling of despair. The national 4-H pledge comes to mind as I think about encouraging others, "I pledge my Head to clearer thinking, my Heart to greater loyalty, my Hands to larger service, and my Health to better living, for my club, my community, my country, and my world." I might edit these well-known words to include, "my soul" as another objective with which to use the "4 Hs" as I lead souls to Salvation.

Personally, I would love to be able to have a grandchild bounce on my lap and enjoy the glow of Kyle and Nicole as they experience parenthood. I would love to see my wife enjoy playing with little grandbabies as she was robbed of this rich experience with our kids as my physicality declined. Of course, I continue to have my daily goal of watching waves pound against the beautiful Emerald Isle sandy shoreline as I sit under a clear blue sky working on my tan while in my mind I am running down the beach. Some things never change!

My final desire is to live long enough to see that ALS has a cure in the near future. Every year, medical advancements are made in other arenas including cancer, heart disease, Parkinson, and other chronic and terminal ailments. I would love to know that funding research has paid off and that familial ALS can be eradicated and non-familial ALS be successfully treated before rendering patients incapable of taking the steps to enjoy a long and fruitful life.

Dr. Richard Bedlack, a Duke University neurologist, is aggressively working, "To empower people with this disease to live longer and better lives and to have a greater role in research." As the television show X-Files' "Fox Mulder" of ALS, Dr. Bedlack, a flamboyant and super intelligent physician, explores reports of unexplained ALS reversals and has documented numerous factual reversals. Through his continued work and research by others in the community, I would love to see this expanded to more patients.

In the September 2017 journal, PLOS One, Dr. Mike Falvo noted that by using a new technique focused on mitochondrial DNA (mtDNA), they have "evidence that mitochondrial dysfunction is involved in the pathology" of Gulf War illnesses. In layman's terms, the Gulf War veterans' genes suggest DNA damage. Perhaps we are on the threshold of a breakthrough of determining specific causes, downstream preventions, and cures... Most recently, the VA approved the use of Radicava (edaravone) for veteran ALS patients as a treatment option. In clinical trials, patients experienced a slower decline in the loss of physical function when using Radicava according to an article by Carolina Henriques in the December 4, 2017 edition of ALS New Today magazine. This is great news!

With hope for cures constantly on our minds, allow me to close with a modified version of a quote made famous by nineteenth century German philosopher Friedrich Nietzsche who put life's challenges in perspective saying, "What doesn't kill me makes me stronger."

Glory to God,

Randy and Kim Hebert

Thomas P. Gill

Randy, Kim & Kyle at the end of Randy's Way

Summer 2017

THE MARINES' PRAYER

Almighty Father, whose command is over all and whose love never fails, make me aware of Thy presence and obedient to Thy will. Keep me true to my best self, guarding me against dishonesty in purpose in deed and helping me to live so that I can face my fellow Marines, my loved ones and Thee without shame or fear. Protect my family. Give the will to do the work of a Marine and to accept my share of responsibilities with vigor and enthusiasm. Grant me the courage to be proficient in my daily performance. Keep me loyal and faithful to my superiors and to the duties my country and the Marine Corps have entrusted to me. Make me considerate of those committed to my leadership. Help me to wear my uniform with dignity, and let it remind me daily of the traditions which I must uphold.

If I am inclined to doubt; steady my faith; if I am tempted, make me strong to resist; if I should miss the mark, give me the courage to try again. Guide me with the light of truth and grant me wisdom by which I may understand the answer to my prayer. Amen

Blessed Darkness

"…We often reflect on times in our lives that do not make sense, that resurface emotional pain beyond measure. The death of a love one, a divorce or diagnosis of cancer can if we allow, cause us to question God's plan for our lives. We must believe to wait and trust in God's timing and plan for each one of us. Help us to always trust You God and to remember that You are always in control of everything! We must trust and believe especially in the darkest times to believe we are never alone, that You are always with us. We must trust that even in the most painful seasons of our lives that **You our Lord do not make mistakes**. Every second of every day we must remember that You already have designed our lives before conception to the last detail. God, we know You did not promise us life without pain. But you did promise it would all work out for our good. … Guide us to have unconditional blind faith in the darkness. Guide us to believe and trust that Your mercy and forgiveness will always give us the hope we need to get through the difficult times. Help us to remember that there are difficult times and painful seasons that You allow us to go through. Guide us to be patient, slow to anger and wait on Your timing. Carry us through difficult times that we don't understand, lead us to Your heavenly light. Guide us, for we trust You. You are the light in the blessed darkness. In God's name we pray.   Amen"

Reprinted with permission from Betty Thompson, RN

Delivered at Swansboro UMC, January 14, 2018

A REFLECTION

So, how did I come to be in Randy's world and more importantly why did God place this opportunity in my hands? People who know me would likely say I am a Christian and hopefully a good man. I guarantee that after meeting Randy and writing this story I have become better at both – not perfect by any stretch as my wife will attest - just better.

I certainly was not planning to write a memoir, especially of someone I did not even know. I had recently retired to Emerald Isle to enjoy the beach, golf, and my family. Ironically, over the past year I had published a novel set in the Emerald Isle area with a second almost finished which more prominently includes the entire North Carolina Crystal Coast. However, these were cathartic releases and fun to write – I did not consider myself an author. I also volunteer with the island Turtle Patrol and voluntarily manage a zone of the island's Neighborhood Watch. Interestingly, Randy's sister-in-law, Dale, is the Emerald Isle Turtle Patrol Program Coordinator and Randy's wife, Kim, is one of my Neighborhood Watch Block Captains. But I did not know these three people were related and had only met Dale.

One rainy December morning I visited Kim at her house to pick up a Neighborhood Watch report and keep her from having to come out in the storm. Like many places on the island, the back door is where you go if you are friends, and well, I wasn't, so I climbed up the front steps, stepped over the locked gate, and rang the bell. In what I know now as typical Kim fashion, after inviting me to use the back steps in the future, she invited me in and asked if I would like to meet Randy. Frankly, I was busy, it was rainy, and I said, "Of course." Seriously, five minutes later I fell in love with Randy Hebert. If you get the opportunity to meet Randy, I bet you will too.

I was introduced to Randy as he sat in his wheelchair in their beautiful kitchen being attended to by one of his wonderful nurses. Quickly I learned I could ask and answer any question or comment, to or from Randy. Kim or the nurse would use their alphabet system Randy and his father designed. I was fascinated. Randy introduced himself and explained he had retired as a young Marine major because of his illness and had been living like this for twenty-two years.

What Randy and Kim didn't know is that I am also a retired officer, have a debilitating illness that at times has kept me from walking, or at best caused me to shuffle like an old man. They also didn't know I had recently retired from a second career in healthcare where I was intimately involved with chronically ill dialysis patients across the spectrum of the disease. Seeing Randy in a wheelchair was a little more intimidating than I was used to, but not much.

As we talked for a few minutes, I joked about my ailment demonstrating how slow I walked while serving as a military commander, trying to be in charge. A few weeks later we learned we are from the same part of the world; Randy from rural Taylors, South Carolina outside Greenville while I grew up about two hours north in the small town of Statesville, North Carolina, just north of Charlotte. On the island we live a short bike ride apart. And, we both grew up in large Catholic families wearing our hair long on our shoulders; *popping wheelies* on string rays with sound effect playing cards stuck in our bike spokes; playing Army with siblings and friends in the kudzu covered woods; running carelessly invisible behind the mosquito fogger truck in the late 1960s; and staying outside from morning until time for dinner - it was safer then because neighbors watched out for each other.

After talking with Randy for a bit, Kim asked, "Did you write *The Bridge* and if so, what led you to write it?" I embarrassingly realized she was asking me and I responded positively.

Kim said, "I have tried to encourage Randy to write a book. I think he has a lot to say. Would you be interested?"

I was stunned, flattered, and quite honestly, scared. I really didn't know what to say, which as most people who know me, is not usually an issue. I had just met them and hadn't even published my second book. *Randy couldn't write it for sure,* and in my heart, *I knew this story needed to be told.* I remember responding that I was honored and excited to be asked and I would need to think about it, ask my "boss" spelled WIFE about tackling this new project, and pray about it – not necessarily in that order.

A secret I am sharing with you only -- I knew I was going to write this book before I left their home. I was unsure how, or if, I could pull this off. But, I would try.

A week later, after praying and talking to several confidants who thought this would be a great project, I met with Randy and Kim and introduced them to our draft outline and title, *Randy's Way.* They loved it and I began.

I hope you enjoyed reading *Randy's Way* as much as I enjoyed meeting Randy's family, friends, and supporters across the island, states, and country. Through famous people like former Presidential candidate, Mr. Ross Perot, and Generals Sturdevant and Arick, to other Marines who put their lives on the line with Randy, we captured a story that provides everyone, not only patients suffering from terminal or chronic diseases, with a wonderful Christian example of how to enjoy life while aggressively fighting earthly roadblocks that lead down the path to everlasting life.

Regardless of your faith, or even lack of faith, we hope by joining our journey you will receive a renewed passion for life and the beauty every minute provides. I am reminded of the doctors who said Randy would be dead in three years and others who suggested I might not be up to the task of writing this story. To both groups I offer the following, first written by English author Walter Bagehot, in an essay on Shakespeare, "The greatest pleasure in life is doing what people say you cannot do." During World War II, the Prime Minister of England, Winston Churchill, put it more concisely when he said, "Never, never, never give up."

Tom

GLOSSARY

AGENT ORANGE. An herbicide used by the U.S. military in Vietnam. It caused health problems like the Gulf War toxic cocktails.

AIDE-DE-CAMP. According to Wikipedia, an aide-de-camp is a French expression meaning *"helper." In the military, it is a personal assistant to a senior officer.*

AMTRACK. Marines call them "amtracks," which comes from their original designation, "amphibious tractor." They are amphibious troop transports of the United States Marine Corps.

ATROPHY. Per Merriam-Webster, "a decrease in size or wasting away of a body part or tissue."

BOBBY HEBERT. The "Cajun Cannon, "Hebert played quarterback in the United States Football League and National Football League from 1983 to 1996 including the New Orleans Saints and Atlanta Falcons.

BLINKING OUT. A term Charlie Pake lovingly used when Randy wanted to communicate and no one was paying attention.

BLITZKRIEG. Warfare method using a concentration of armored infantry and close air support to break through the opponent's defense with short, fast, surprise attacks.

CHAPLAIN OF THE SENATE. According to Wikipedia, The Chaplain of the United States Senate is chosen to "perform ceremonial, symbolic, and pastoral duties which include opening Senate sessions with a prayer or coordinating the delivery of the prayer by guest chaplains recommended by members of the Senate."

COMMANDER'S CUP. Throughout most military branches, a challenge between smaller groups of members within a unit commanded by a Colonel or equivalent involving physical activity as well as performance within their specialty.

D-DAY. Normally thought as the World War II Allied invasion of Normandy on June 6, 1944; however, it may be any day of special significance, as one marking an important event or goal.

DON/DONNING. To put on… MOPP gear.

E.F. HUTTON. A 20th century American financier who co-founded the financial firm by his name. Commercials in the late 1970s often commented, "When E.F. Hutton talks, people listen."

EZ KEYS. According to their website, EZ Keys is designed for users who have at least a third-grade reading level and cannot speak, or for users who speak and desire adapted computer access. Users with a wide range of disabilities find EZ Keys simple to operate and essential to everyday communication. EZ Keys allows the literate user to do everything from typing a letter to engaging in conversation with a friend. World-renowned astrophysicist Stephen Hawking used the software to communicate, write papers, and deliver lectures around the world.

FEEDING TUBE. Also called a "G-Tube," this is a medical device which provides nutrition to individuals who cannot obtain nutrition by mouth and/or are unable to swallow.

FOG OF WAR. Term used during several past wars to describe challenges due to the complexities such as communication and supply chain.

FOX VEHICLE. During Desert Storm, provided real time nuclear, biological and chemical detection for battlefield combatants.

FORT FISHER. Civil War era fort commanded by General Louis Hebert near Kure Beach, North Carolina.

FREEDOM HIGHWAY. Name given to North Carolina Highway 24 in the proximity of Camp Lejeune and New River Marine Corps Air Station.

G-DAY: Ground attack of Iraq on February 24, 1991.

GILLIGAN'S ISLAND "THREE HOUR TOUR." Popular 1970's television show about castaways who innocently started out on a three-hour tour from Hawaii until they were shipwrecked.

GQ. Formerly Gentlemen's Quarterly, is an international monthly men's magazine providing a forum for men's culture, fashion, style, fitness, and more.

GROUND POUNDER. A military member typically part of the infantry such as in the Marine Corps or Army.

GULF WAR: OPERATION DESERT SHIELD/DESERT STORM. Lasted from August 2, 1990 until February 28, 1991. Codenamed Desert Shield until January 17, 1991 as the troop buildup intensified. Became Desert Storm on January 17, 1991 during the combat phase until over on February 28, 1991.

GULF WAR SYNDROME/DISEASE. According to the Encyclopedia of Britannica, "Cluster of illnesses in veterans of the Persian Gulf War (1990–91) characterized not by any definable medical condition or diagnostic test but by variable and nonspecific symptoms such as fatigue, anxiety, muscle and joint pains, headaches, memory loss, and posttraumatic stress reactions. Gulf War syndrome is believed to be caused by exposure to a class of chemicals known as anticholinesterases.

HUMP. To march, walk, hike, or otherwise engage in long distance traveling by foot for the purposes of waging war or moving materials.

HUMV. High mobility multipurpose wheeled vehicle initially designed for warfare.

ICE BUCKET CHALLENGE. An activity involving the dumping of a bucket of ice and water over a person's head, either by another person or self-administered, to promote awareness of ALS and encourage research donations.

ISLAND OF PATMOS. An Aegean island in the north of Greece's Dodecanese island group where St. John, the theologian, is said to have written the Book of Revelations.

MILITARY RANKS AND TITLES. Exclusive of all ranks, the following are referred to within the book: officers, enlisted members, field grade officer, Private, Lance Corporal, Corporal, Sergeant, Drill Instructor, Master Sergeant, First Sergeant, Sergeant Major, Lieutenant, Captain, Major, Lieutenant Colonel, Colonel, Brigadier General, Major General, General, and Commandant of the Marine Corps.

MONOMELIC AMYOTROPHY. Rare disease in the United States that presents with atrophy of the brain, insomnia, depression, heart problems, tearing of eyes, and other symptoms.

MEECHUM FAMILY. Pat Conroy's dysfunctional Marine family in The Great Santini.

MOPP. Mission Oriented Protective Posture pronounced "mop" is protective gear used by military personnel in a toxic environment.

MP. Abbreviation for Military Police.

PROMISE KEEPERS. Promise Keepers is self-described as "a Christ-centered organization dedicated to introducing men to Jesus Christ as their Savior and Lord, helping them to grow as Christians."

PYRIDOSTIGMINE BROMIDE (PB) PILL. Taken for anti-nerve agent protection.

Y2K. Anticipated computer challenges resulted because programmers reduced the four-digit year to two digits making the year 2000 indistinguishable from the year 1900.

RED HORSE SQUADRON. Like the Seabees, it is the U.S. Air Force's construction component. It takes its name from Rapid Engineer Deployable Heavy Operational Repair Squadron.

SADDAM HUSSEIN. An Iraqi dictator who waged war against Iran and invaded Kuwait resulting in the world's coalition forces defeating him during Desert Storm.

SARIN NERVE AGENT. Highly toxic, colorless, and odorless chemical.

SEABEES. U.S. Navy construction force. Originally took its name from the heterograph "C.B." which stood for Construction Battalion.

SEAL. Sea, air, and land teams are the U.S. Navy's premiere special operations force.

TOXIC COCKTAIL. Used to describe the Persian Gulf War and current day poisonous situations around the world. In this case, specifically referring to the burning oil fields along with the toxic chemical weapons known to have been stored and used by Saddam Hussein in Iraq.

TRACHEOTOMY. Also referred to as a trach; a surgical procedure that requires an incision in the neck and trachea so a tube can be placed in the opening of the throat to restore or allow airflow to the lungs.

UPSTATE. The westernmost part of South Carolina situated between Charlotte NC and Atlanta Georgia.

VETERANS AFFAIRS (VA). The federal department responsible for administering a variety of service members' benefits including healthcare, education, home loans, rehabilitation and more.

WASHINGTON D.C. MALL. A national park in downtown Washington D.C. with many monuments, museums, and memorials.

WOODSTOCK. 1969 music festival near the rural White Lake hamlet in New York. Attracted over 400,000 people.

ACKNOWLEDGEMENTS

It is impossible to thank everyone who provided such tremendous support in the crafting of Randy's Way. Reliving Randy's past fifty years through family and friends, while emphasizing the past quarter century, was enjoyable and hopefully creates a thematic reflection that provides a source of inspiration for anyone suffering life's challenges. To Randy's parents, siblings, children, in-laws, childhood friends and so many others, I offer my deepest appreciation for your willingness to be interviewed, some pleasant and others perhaps less so, as we unearthed long forgotten stories and anecdotes. Thanks also to friends who provided photographs, including the Tideland News (Berry-Bates photo) to honor Randy and Kim and glorify God. To my new Emerald Isle neighbors, friends, and Randy's Marine Corps buddies, thank you for reliving the past and allowing my invasion of your privacy and personal lives. Each memory warmed Randy's heart as I reported back to Randy and Kim throughout the entire process. Sincere thanks to the many beta readers and editors, too numerous to name. For those who offered encouragement when others thought this too daunting of a challenge and to those who read the early manuscript versions and offered honest feedback and constructive criticism – thank you! Each provided inspiration helping ensure I delivered on this promise. Incorporating just the right touches, thanks goes to Simone Weithers for her beautiful cover design. Finally, my deepest appreciation to my family who coached me through this journey. Your unwavering help, love, and confidence made this possible.

With deepest love and appreciation,

Tom

ABOUT THE AUTHOR

Tom Gill began writing after careers as an Air Force officer and health care executive. His first novel, *The Bridge*, and its sequel, *Return to Emerald Isle*, are summer beach romance reads set primarily in North Carolina's Crystal Coast and are filled with mystery, suspense, and humor. Tom actively shares his writing passion across North Carolina with students, libraries, and writers' groups; assists with numerous military transition programs; volunteers on various island committees; and finds time to play golf, when not on the beach. Tom also serves on various boards including Fire Leadership Foundation, a national scholarship granting and mentoring program for underprivileged students. Tom and his high school sweetheart live on Emerald Isle, North Carolina, where they enjoy being close to their granddaughter, two adult daughters, son-in-law, and their alma mater, East Carolina University.

Made in United States
Orlando, FL
26 April 2022

17219839R00133